NAVIES, PETROL AND CHOCOLATE

WHY UKRAINE MATTERS

P. PHILLIPS GODSTON

Navies, Petrol and Chocolate: Why Ukraine Matters

Peter Phillips Godston

Third Edition (March 2021)

ISBN-13: 978-1537752761   ISBN-10: 1537752766

Nonfiction > Reference > Military

History > Europe > General

Business & Economics > Exports & Imports

Political Science > International Relations

TABLE OF CONTENTS

Introduction

Navies, petrol and chocolate. Those words were appropriate
in 2016, when I set out to write a book about Ukraine. Russian
troops and surrogates had recently occupied parts of Ukraine,
developments that some claimed were justified given the warm water naval port in Crimea. Territorial seas adjacent to Crimea
also contained deep water oil reserves, which might be helpful
to Russia as Putin's own oil reserves were being emptied years
into the future.

Also, the sitting president of Ukraine, Petro Poroshenko,
had made his fortune in the chocolate industry, resulting in
substantial personal credibility across the board and specifically enabling acquisition of a television channel and the funding of multiple political campaigns. Ultimately, chapters bear-
ing the words "navies, petrol and chocolate" went well beyond
the immediately obvious.

The navies chapter chronicled the journey of Russia's navy
from Peter the Great's founding of a deep water navy in the late
1600's, through the Soviet Union's unrealistic ship building aspirations leading up to World War 2, and the Soviet's ultimate
relative success with naval technology and naval funding after

the Great Patriotic War and as a result of the embarrassing US blockade opposing the Soviet Navy during the Cuban Missile Crisis of the early 1960's.

The petrol chapter delineated the influence of oil sources in driving United States policy in the Middle East as well as some discussion of the flirtation that various oil companies had with Ukraine regarding deep water oil development, opportunities that evaporated for Ukraine upon Russian occupation of Crimea.

The chocolate chapter was perhaps the most ambitious of all. In addition to a hasty outline of Petro Poroshenko's commercial career and rise to political influence, "Chocolate" provided a cursory review of the development of commerce and government in Ukraine from pre-history to present day.

There are multiple reasons for publishing a subsequent edition of a book. Sometimes passing events compel an update (my rationale for a Second Edition of <u>Navies</u>, <u>Petrol</u> <u>and</u> <u>Chocolate</u>, published shortly after Donald Trump's election). Joe Biden's election as the next President of the United States justifies a third edition, even if there were no other reason for an update.

Sometimes there are developments about the way an audience for a book might perceive certain important conclusions: the groundswell of public opinion regarding global warming and petrol consumption has grown much stronger since publication of our

Second Edition. This groundswell might discourage action supporting Ukraine's development of its petroleum and natural gas reserves, even if we can assume commercial markets will welcome Ukraine oil and gas products irrespective of protestors suggesting all petroleum development and consumption should cease immediately.

Certainly, Hunter Biden's involvement with Burisma, the Ukraine natural gas company, justifies a few paragraphs regarding government and business ethics in a third edition, even if Donald Trump hadn't been forced to endure an impeachment proceeding due to the President's call to the Ukraine president about an investigation regarding Hunter's involvement.

Petro Poroshenko's considerable fortune was diminished during his tenure as president of Ukraine, even as his control of commercial chocolate interests continued. Ultimately, the Ukraine people chose a comedian with no political experience, Volodimir Zelenskiy, who played the president on television, to serve as president instead. While we will leave "chocolate" in the book and chapter titles, we will certainly review Zelenskiy's rise to power and his record since achieving office.

My own immersion in technology tools also justifies augmentation to all three of these titled chapters. Geographic Information Systems have continued to evolve and have a dramatic impact on the operation of navies and naval weaponry. Big data tools enhance understanding of petroleum and natural gas products and the markets that Ukraine might penetrate with related commercial efforts. Block chain technology impacts many industries, although perhaps not as dramatically (yet) as some have predicted, but block chain offers an opportunity to deliver resources to the African continent, a higher priority than Ukraine in various United States policy minds and where cocoa beans, the primary raw material for chocolate, are primarily sourced.

Sometimes an author's thinking also expands. I admit that finally reading Jared Diamond's excellent book, <u>Guns</u>, <u>Germs</u> <u>and</u> <u>Steel</u>: <u>The</u> <u>Fate</u> <u>of</u> <u>Human</u> <u>Societies</u>, in the early days of 2021, has inspired a more scientific examination of some of Ukraine's development, even if conclusions revealed in my collegiate experiences with Russian and broader Western Civilization may be sufficient to dissect causal dynamics and propose policy improvements.

I am grateful to the Army and Intelligence Communities for fueling many foundational ideas leading to this book, and to my professors at Johns Hopkins University and Harvard Business School. I am also grateful to various members of these communities who reviewed and commented on early versions, driving (I hope) more accuracy and sharpening my conclusions. I am also grateful to my ex-wife, many friends and two daughters for the support and affection that enabled what became a bit of a crusade here. Ultimately, none of this was possible without these people. Of course, any errors contained here are mine and mine alone. Enjoy!

Empire

Although Peter the Great subjugated Ukraine at Poltava, and
the struggle of empires may cloud the roots of Ukraine identity,
Kievan Rus proved a center of commerce and culture for hundreds
of years. After World War II, the great powers drew new national boundaries, including the Soviet Socialist Republic of
Ukraine, where Kievan culture and religion reemerged. The
strength of the Ukraine nation state surprised some when the Soviet Union dissolved in 1991.

Sometime in March 1709, Peter the Great and his secret
wife, Catherine, conceived one of their two surviving children.
Theirs' is a love story that has survived the cobwebs of history: his mother forced Peter to marry a woman of noble birth
early in his reign, but as he matured, the man who would be Tsar
of the Russias cast aside his first wife.

Peter met Catherine some years before, in a cloud of palace
intrigue. Marta was a beautiful Polish Lithuanian, who had experience traveling with armies and consorting with powerful men.
Although the introduction was made through Alexander Menshikov,
a man who aspired to influence the young Tsar, and whose palace

still attracts tourists to St Petersburg for its architectural beauty and artifacts from the early 18th century, the relationship stood on its own, and only further tightened Menshikov's relationship with the Tsar.

Marta adopted Orthodox Christianity, changed her name to Catherine Alexayevna, and (along with Menshikov's new wife) proceeded to accompany her husband on his many military excursions. Thus, we don't know for certain where Catherine and Peter were on a map in June, 1709, when tactical positioning against Ukraine was being finalized.

They may very well have been visiting a little cabin near St Petersburg, where they lived while the palace was being built. Legend suggests the two lived together there as if they were "an ordinary couple," with Catherine cooking and tending children (a first child would not be born until December in that year). Peter tended to the garden and oversaw the construction of the grand new capital, St Petersburg, which was essentially being reclaimed from a swamp.

In any event, we can imagine Sheremetev's scouts reporting information regarding the army of the Swedish King Charles, including details about his ties to the Ukrainian leader, Ivan Mazeppa. Ukraine was called a Hetmanate at this point in history, and a substantial amount of Mazeppa's influence and wealth had accrued to him due to his service to the Russian Tsar. But it had become clear to Mazeppa that Peter planned to subjugate the Hetmanate more completely to Russian authoritarian rule. And so it was that Mazeppa secretly allied himself with the Swedish King.

In the years leading up to the final battle, large numbers of Russian and Swedish casualties were incurred across many battles, with more losses and casualties absorbed by the Russians, but with leadership on either side expecting ultimate victory. In late June, Peter reinforced Russian forces at Poltava against some remaining 20,000 Swedes. As Peter's luck had it, the previously impervious Swedish king was wounded in skirmishes, casting doubt within a force that would require all of Charles' tactical genius, overwhelming confidence among his troops and valiant combat from the Cossacks of Ivan Mazeppa.

Perhaps a contextual pause is appropriate here. We were 70 years before to the American Revolution, although historians note that Mardi Gras was already being celebrated in Louisiana. The New England colonies had made a reputation for ship building, while the middle American colonies fostered trade and the southern colonies provided excellent farming. Wealthy colonists acquired substantial land, but most people arrived as an indentured servant (a contractual agreement that offered passage in exchange for a 7-year period of service).

China was at the apex of its imperial period under the Qing Dynasty, while Emperor Nakamikado ascended to the throne of Japan in that year. Alamgir was hailed Caliph in India, where Hindu's were both taxed and poorly treated, as were other non-Muslims.

In 1709, Germany was the Syria of its day, due to repeated invasions from the French. A substantial number of Germans (13,000 poor Palatines) emigrated to England to escape this violence and many hoping to travel from there to the new world, causing a significant political stir about immigration. The War of Spanish Succession was underway and the Great Northern War between Russia and Sweden was nearing its end.

Thanks to victories in the Thirty Year's and Second Northern War, Sweden had subjugated Denmark and otherwise controlled most of the Baltic/Northern Europe. Charles XII assumed the throne early but quickly proved himself worthy of leading the Swedish state. Peter the Great was a larger than life figure, something of a mix between Elon Musk and Michael Jordan, standing nearly 7 feet tall, leading his forces into combat, enjoying the great wealth of the Russian Romanov royal family along with absolute power in the territory he controlled.

The battle at Poltava has inspired innumerable works of art. Multiple paintings were created across hundreds of years and throughout Europe. Tchaikovsky wrote an opera (Mazeppa).

Lord Byron, Alexander Pushkin and Victor Hugo wrote poems. More recently, Swedish heavy metal band "Sabaton" wrote a hit song.

Although January of 1709 witnessed the coldest day in 500 years (or at least for a hundred years), on the morning of July 8th, 1709, the weather was unusually hot. Charles had kept the Russian fortress at Poltava under siege since May, but Peter the

Great's arrival with reinforcements was not answered on the Swedish side (Swedish General Lewenhaupt was delayed due to the anti-Swedish Sandomierz Confederation in Poland).

In preparation for the battle, the Russians opted to build six new forts between Yakovetski and Budyschenski forest lines and four additional redoubts to create a "t" shape on the battlefield. Swedish forces attacked before all earthworks were complete, but 4000 Russian soldiers had their benefit, with Menshikov's 10,000 cavalry behind them.

Charles' plan of attack was to throw four columns of infantry and six columns of cavalry past the redoubts before daybreak, but his cavalry got lost in the dark. In addition, instead of bypassing them according to Charles' plan, Swedes quickly over ran two of the redoubts, but stalled at the third. Thus, Swedish General Roos and a third of the Swedish infantry were halted, while the rest waited for the cavalry to arrive. During the wait, Russian cavalry, Skoropadsky's Cossacks and twenty-three Russian infantry battalions were able to force the surrender of Roos forces.

Thus, Swedish forces were still waiting for Roos just before 9:45, when Peter the Great led 42 battalions in the attack, under cover of his much larger collection of cannon (55 three-pounders plus another 32 on the fort, to the Swedish four (4) cannon).

Barely able to gather his cavalry squadrons, [Swedish General] Creutz tried to advance on the right flank, but the Russian battalions were able to form into hollow squares, while Menshikov's cavalry outflanked the Swedes and attacked them from the rear. At this point, the Swedish assault had disintegrated, and no longer had organized bodies of troops to oppose the Russian infantry or cavalry. (Wikipedia, "Battle of Poltava")

On the Russian side, Peter reported three near misses: one bullet passed through his hat; one hit his saddle; while a third reportedly damaged the gold cross on the Tsar's chest. Charles was fortunate to escape with a few soldiers and his life. He fell to an assassin's bullet 9 years later. Mazeppa escaped with Charles, dying of old age a short time after the battle (in the Turkish fortress at Bendery). In 2009, Ukrainian President Viktor Yushchenko revealed that his family may be related to Mazeppa.

Kiev is thought to have existed in the 700's AD as a Slavic settlement. The city grew to an apex as center of Kievan Rus in 10th Century (due in part to trade on the Dniepr river) and flourished until being crushed during the Mongol invasion in 1240. Kievan Rus officially became Christian in 988AD with baptism of Vladimir the Great (who preceded to baptize his subjects), although we are told Saint Andrew converted thousands in his travels through the Kiev region and as far north as Novgorod in the First Century.

The Christian (orthodox) faith has been a unifying theme in Ukraine since those days, although Soviet Russians converted most Ukraine churches to barracks and libraries after consolidating power, even completely demolishing the remarkable St Michael's church in Kiev in a fit of anti-religious fervor. St Michael's has since been rebuilt.

##

Several hundred years after the founding of the Roman Republic and three hundred years before the birth of Christ, a petty king perfected infantry phalanx and cavalry wedge tactics, then suffered death to an assassin. (Richard A Gabriel. Phillip II of Macedon. Potomac Books: Washington, DC, 2010) His son assumed the throne at twenty and proceeded to earn the reputation as the most successful military commander in history. Alexander the Great (323 BC) in turn died at an early age, after granting property to many of his soldiers (and coopting many of his conquests to Hellenic culture and governance). While his was one of the largest empires in history, his conquests went south and east of Macedonia, and never touched land that would become Kievan Rus or Ukraine.

The Roman Republic expanded to control most of Italy and lands touching the Mediterranean before the birth of Christ, reaching well into Europe, Turkey and Egypt as an Empire, before the city itself was sacked by the Visigoths in 410AD. While Rome held lands at the base of the Black Sea, Kievan Rus did not extend this far south.

At their apex, Goths held lands that became Southern Kievan Rus, but they too stopped south and west of Kievan Rus, collaps-

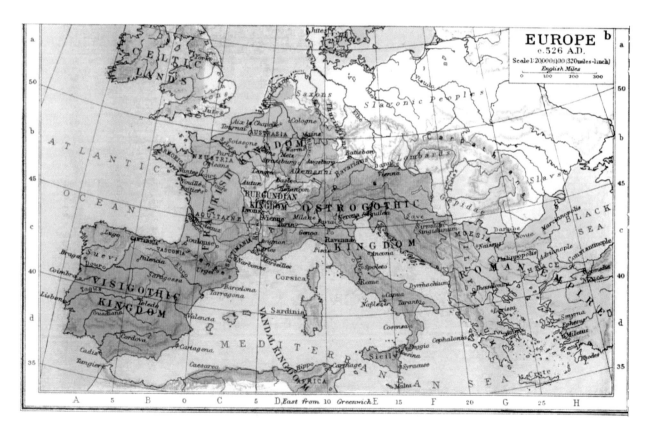

ing in 700AD under Arab and Berber attacks. Maps that describe the era of the Goths reference "Slavonic Peoples" holding land across some of modern Germany and all Eastern Europe.

Legend suggests that that Chuds, Eastern Slavs, Merias, Ve-
ses, and Krivichs invited Rurik and his Varangian tribe to establish order among them. Rurik founded a dynasty that ruled
Kievan Rus, the Grand Duchy of Moscow and the Tsardom of Russia
until the 17th Century. (Wikipedia) Evidently there was a Roe-
rik who had received lands from Emperor Louis, but began plun-
dering neighboring lands, which enraged the Emperor who stripped
all his possessions. The date of the stripping corresponds with
the invitation to Kievan Rus described above. DNA places Rurik's closest living relatives on the coast of Finland among
Swedish-speaking Finns.

Accomplishments of the Rurik dynasty include Christianiza-
tion of Rus, founding of the glorious Kiev Pecharsk Monastery
where Christianity thrived for centuries (then survived under
Communism), establishment of a written legal code "Rossiskaya
Pravda" and recognition as a kingdom from the Pope and the Holy
Roman Emperor.

Rurik lived in Ladoga and Novgorod, remaining in power until his death in 879. He was succeeded by Oleg, who moved the
capital of Rus from Novgorod to Kiev, from where he launched a
raid on Constantinople. Oleg's accomplishments included serving
as army commander under Rurik, then under his own reign, establishing a trade treaty with Byzantium and keeping Rurik's son,
Igor, safe. Oleg died in 912 and was succeeded by Igor, who

ruled until his assassination in 945. There are disputes among historians about whether the Igor who succeeded Oleg was Rurik's son and regarding how quickly Oleg assumed the throne after Rurik's death.

Igor's son Sviatoslav assumed power upon Igor's assassination, finally being crowned in 964. Sviatoslav defeated numerous tribes, pressuring Khazaria and the First Bulgarian Empire until they collapsed. Although his mother accepted Christianity in the court of Constantine, Sviatoslav remained a pagan until his death in an ambush in 972, at the age of 30. Sviatoslav was the first ruler of Kievan Rus with a Slavic name; names of previous rulers were of Norse origin.

Sviatoslav had several wives and evidently had children through them, but his successor Vladimir was born to Malusha "a woman of indeterminate origin." (Wikipedia) Sviatoslav attacked Volga Bulgaria and sacked Kerch, Crimea. Sviatoslav's removal of the Khazar imperial power enabled Rus domination of north-south trade routes through the steppe and across the Black Sea.

Sviatoslav's son Yaropolk received Kiev from his father and was able to consolidate and maintain power until 980, when Vladimir (son from Malusha) enlisted Varangian mercenaries, forced the daughter of a Polotsk prince to marry him and seized Kiev.

After receiving promises of peace, Yaropolk traveled to negotiations, where, on the road, he was ambushed and killed by two Varangians.

After retaking Novgorod and seizing the throne, Vladimir consolidated his empire and converted everyone to Christianity in 988. Remarkably, Vladimir installed his successor in Turov at eight years old, subsequently arranging his marriage with the daughter of the Polish king.

Kievan Rus

The successor, also named Sviatopolk, attempted to overthrow Vladimir and, upon failure, was thrown in prison. Upon learning of his death after Vladimir's passing in 1015, Sviatopolk seized the throne, killing his three brothers to reduce opposition.

Vladimir's youngest son, Yaroslav, defeated Sviatopolk in 1019, subsequently codifying legal customs that became known as Rossiskaya Pravda. Yaroslav ruled until 1054, when his oldest son, Iziaslav, became Grand Prince of Kiev. Iziaslav is credited with founding the Kiev Pechersk Monastery, giving an entire mountain to Antonite monks who had founded a monastery in a cave there. Although intrigue resulted in his three sons rule as the Yaroslavichi triumvirate for twenty years, Iziaslav was able to enlist the assistance of the German king Henry IV (the Holy Roman Emperor), Polish King Boleslaw and Pope Gregory VII. The Pope sent him a crown in 1075, establishing his title as King of Rus, after which he took Kiev… dying shortly thereafter.

Sviatoslav II ruled Kiev for several years, commissioning several theological works. Vsevolod I also ruled for only a few years then was succeeded by Sviatopolk II, who ruled until 1093. These short reigns were contested, and protests against the unpopular princes were common. Vladimir II reigned until 1125, followed by Mstislav the last ruler of a unified Rus. And so the fractured Rus was conquered (Kiev sacked) by the Mongols in 1240.

In his second installment of political history, which he calls Political Order and Political Decay, (Profile Books: London, 2015) Francis Fukuyama places blame: "The Mongols destroyed the nascent state formed around Kiev Rus…" (p239).

Ghengis Khan organized his skilled archer-horsemen, penetrating well into China, Turkistan, Afghanistan and southeastern

Europe (1240-1370). Stubborn resistance was answered with decisive retribution: cities leveled, populations erased and war prisoners used as front line defense. Weapon innovations included catapults and explosives (Robert Sullivan, et. al. <u>The World's Great Civilizations</u>. Life Books: New York, 2012 p. 70). Ruthless domination lost momentum through the centuries, however. Although it was from the Mongol authority that the immediate predecessor to Mikhael Romanov received his patent for ruling Russia, after sacking Kiev and ruling for a little over a hundred years, the Mongol empire fractured and was absorbed in the broader conflicts of Europe and Asia.

The Ottoman Empire, ruled by Caliph, conqueror of Constantinople, considered itself the heir of Rome, its ruler only answerable to God. Osman I's reign began in 1230... although its zenith was under Suleiman, who reigned until 1566.. stagnation and decline began just before 1700. The empire was finally abolished in 1922, although the country that replaced it, Turkey, survives as a democracy today, albeit with challenges to that very democracy from both democratically elected leadership and the military, which attempted a coup in July, 2016.

Beginning later and ending sooner, the Byzantine Empire (527 to 565 AD) set an example of state conversion to Christianity "Preaching and conducting worship in the vernacular... Cyril and Methodius were very successful in converting tribes of slavs…" Willner, et al, <u>Let's Review: Global History and Geography</u>. Barron's: Brooklyn, 2002 (p. 285) Cyril created the Cyrillic alphabet although various historians credit people living in early Ukraine with some of the earliest formation of language, in pursuit of building tools as well as planning and producing food.

To the north and east of Rus lands lie Polish territories. Poland and Lithuania explored various state partnerships, beginning in the 1400's, finally striking a "permanent" Union of Lublin in 1549. Polish-Lithuania became a commonwealth, instituting perhaps the most democratic of European governments in the 17th Century and controlling much of Ukraine after the Mongol empire crumbled. In 1648, however, Ukrainian Cossacks rebelled against the Polish-Lithuanians.

Fukuyama attributes the Mongols for cutting "Russia off from trade and intellectual exchange with Byzantium, the Middle East, and Europe and undermining Russia's Byzantine-Roman legal tradition." (IBID p 239) During what some call the appanage period, the Metropolitan in Kiev governed much of Eastern Orthodoxy, but political authority on the land was increasingly divided among petty nobility, undermining governing and economic unity. ("The Appanage Period," <u>http://www.myhistro.com/story/the-founding-and-medieval-history-of-russia/9874#!the-appanage-period-24224</u>) Thus, there was no development of a deeply rooted feudalism that provided strong local government… no time to build the fortified castles that were critical to the protection of feudal power." (Fukuyama, p. 239)

Ukraine groups alternatively sought protection from the Russian Tsar (Treaty of Perayaslav) and the Swedish King. Some hundred years before, rivals including Simeon I appealed for a patent and title, "Prince of Moscow." Simeon won out against the rivals, although he and his sons died in the black death a few years later. A boyar in his employ named Andrey Kobyla managed a family of some prominence, served under the reign of Ivan the Terrible then changed their family name to Romanov.

After Ivan the Terrible, leadership of Muscovy languished under Feodor and Boris Godunov. Several Rurik and Gedimin princes were able to expel the Poles from Moscow in 1605, but none were willing to accept the crown when Russia's Zemsky Zabor offered it. Mikhail Romanov, then a resident at the Ipatiev Monastery, consented to the title. Mikhail's son was Alexai. One of Alexai's sons (via his second wife) was Peter, who shared the throne with his sickly brother at the beginning of his reign. This Peter consolidated his throne, began expanding his empire and in 1709 sent forces to Ukraine to confront Charles XII and Ivan Mazeppa.

Ivan Mazeppa studied at Kyivan Mohyla College, then went to Warsaw to study at a Jesuit college there. He attracted the interest of the Polish king when serving at a page at the court of Jan II Casimir Vasa, and was sent by the king to study in Holland, learning gunnery there and traveling on to Germany, Italy, France and the Low Countries (Holland, then the premier commercial center in the world).

The Polish king sent Mazeppa back to Ukraine on various diplomatic missions, returning permanently to live in 1663, in order to help his ailing father. At his father's passing, Mazeppa became hereditary cupbearer of Chernihiv, entering service under Hetman Petro Doroshenko as a squadron commander, where he took part in the Campaign against Poland and served as Doroshenko's chancellor.

During missions to Crimea and Turkey, Mazeppa was fortuitously captured by the Zaporazian Ottoman, then handed to the "left bank Cossacks," Ivan Samoylovich. It was here that Mazeppa came into service of the Russian Tsar, Peter the Great. Mazeppa was installed as new Hetman after the Cossack Council deposed Samoylovich. In this role, he hoped to unify all Ukrainian territories into a state like any other in Europe, while retaining features of the Cossack order. Unfortunately, Mazeppa's support for Peter's many wars undermined his popularity, so that when Peter moved the Metropolitan to Moscow, then abolished the Cossack order and privileges, Mazeppa had limited loyalty among much needed Ukraine allies, to fight back.

Peter the Great dramatically improved the efficiency of the Russian Empire, expanded the territories it held and tightening the authoritarian hold he had on the territories of his empire. Subsequent Tsars continued efforts to expand or at least control the Russian Empire, with mixed success.

Napoleon seized control of France in 1799, riding a tide of European nationalism and French conscription, which vastly increased the size of the Armies representing a state. Napoleon was brilliantly successful in Europe through 1808, although expansion attempts stalled in Russia in 1812, then crumbled at the Battle of Waterloo in 1815. European monarchs lost thrones due to Napoleon, and ideals of the French Revolution were spread throughout. (Willner, Let's Review, p. 374).

In the late 1700's, Poland was more focussed on enemies to the East and North than with Ukraine, including Russia's Tsar Alexander I, victor against Napoleon. Austria, Prussia and Russia subdivided what had been Polish-Latvian territory multiple times, culminating in Russian invasion after the Polish king attempted liberal reforms in 1830. A brief spark of rebellion was crushed by the Russians, whereupon the Polish state ceased to exist (although emigres kept Polish nationality alive in places like Paris).

When Russia defected from the Allied coalition in 1917 due to its Bolshevik revolution, Woodrow Wilson made Poland a component of his crusade to spread democracy, creating the Polish nation in the thirteenth of his fourteen points.

A Pole named Jozef Pilsudski became a popular hero in his home country when the Germans jailed him for insubordination. Thus, in October 1918, a puppet Kingdom of Poland set up by German, Austrio-Hungarian and Russian Empires, ceded control to him, with all local governments set up in the final stages of the war pledging allegiance to the new Polish state.

Of course, previous to this, Ukraine had set up a provisional government and proclaimed itself a republic within the structure of a federated Russia. Unfortunately, Ukraine's Rada government was unable to impose rule on its own people, particularly in the face of the Bolshevik opposition. After splitting into Eastern and Western countries, Ukraine unified and even allied with Poland, but was not able to stop a Soviet armed incursion. Thus, in 1922, Ukraine become one of the original republics in the USSR.

Seventeen years later, Nazi Germany invaded Poland after Stalin and Hitler came to a secret agreement in the Molotov-Ribbentrop Pact. Then, two years after that, Hitler invaded Ukraine as part of a comprehensive attack on the USSR.

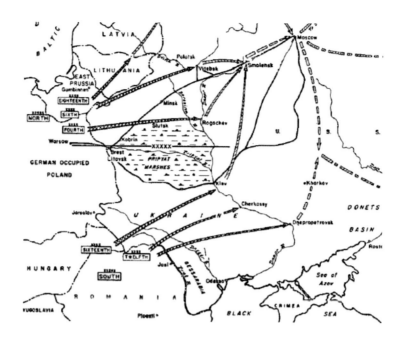

There were Ukraine sympathizers with Nazi Germany:

"With the Soviet massacre of intelligentsia and the great Holod-
omor famine of the 1930s still fresh in mind, there were large

elements of Ukrainians who welcomed the Germans as liberators,

especially in western Ukraine. Some volunteered and joined the

Schutzmannschaft, a German-controlled auxiliary police unit that

helped guard concentration camps and fought against resistance

elements in Ukraine and Byelorussia. Early in the Russo-German

war, about 4,000 Ukrainians operated under German orders to aid

the German war effort. On 28 Apr 1943, a Ukrainian SS unit was

formed, which later became a part of the *Waffen-SS* as the SS Di-

vision "Galizien" and then the *14. Waffen-Grenadier-Division der*

SS; there were claims that these volunteers actively participated in atrocities of the Holocaust." http://ww2db.com/coun-
try/Ukraine

There were Ukrainians who suffered similar persecutions to
that of Jewish peoples elsewhere in Europe: 500,000 were estimated to have perished in German concentration camps. (IBID)
But the vast majority of Ukraine was devoted to defending the
USSR against Nazi Germany:

"…as the second-largest member nation by population in the Soviet Union, Ukrainians made up a large portion of the Soviet
military, and thus sharing a proportional lost in the Russo-German War that lasted between 1941 and 1945: during the war, about
4,500,000 Ukrainians served with the Soviets, and 1,400,000 were
killed in service." (IBID)

The tide began to turn in Karkov, and elsewhere in Eastern
Ukraine:

> On December 19, 1942, the Nazi forces were dislodged from
> the first Ukrainian villages. Kyiv was liberated on Novem-
> ber 6, 1943. In October 1944, the entire Ukrainian terri-
> tory was free from Hitler's forces. Trans Carpathian
> Ukraine was liberated on October 26-28. In November, the
> congress of people's committee in Mukacheve made a resolu-
> tion about the Trans Carpathian withdrawal from Czechoslo-
> vakia and its reunification with Ukraine. The new region
> expanded Ukraine's territory to 577 thousand square miles.
> (Worldwide News Ukraine, http://wnu-ukraine.com/about-
> ukraine/history/soviet-rule-and-world-war/)

After World War II, a new division of Europe included the

Soviet Socialist Republic of Ukraine. Nikita Khruschev was appointed to lead it. Although some called the USSR an Empire, it's driving motivation was a communist ideology, not national imperialism.

The era of empires had ended.

##

While the Nation-State as a concept is alive and well at this writing, a number of non- and quasi-state organizations compete with the State for the loyalty of subjects or citizens. Vladimir Putin calls Russians to serve Mother Russia, the United Kingdom still has its crown, and the United States, our Constitution and flag.

Although nations and even personalities attract loyalty in China and North Korea, those countries, like Kruschev's Soviet Union (but not Vladimir Putin's Russia), still pledge loyalty to a Communist ideology, expecting people to behave (and think) like good Communists.

Some of the world's countries are decisively areligious or, like the United States, profess to separate church and state. But with the ebb of Communist and Socialist ideology worldwide, there has been a surge of Muslim loyalties, in many cases radical. Radical Muslim ideology does not confine itself to a single border, although, like the Islamic Republic of Iran, there are certainly a number of nation states that claim religious defining ideas and loyalty.

Thanks to select verses in Islam's defining document, the Koran, there is a call to fight exploitation and also to establish a broader global "Caliphate." These ideas are dangerous in and of themselves, but coupled with calls to secular violence in the Koran, certainly confuse citizens of Western Democracies, who typically wish to allow freedom of expression and freedom of religion.

We find citizens of other states, even Western ones, adopting Radical Muslim tenets and carrying out independent acts of violence without real recruitment, perhaps even without meeting a member of a terrorist organization or opposing Nation-state. While many "failing states" may adhere to Muslim ideology, perhaps some of the most successful "non-states" adhere to it.

While some Muslim ideas may confuse non-Muslims, and do not drive the behavior of most followers of The Prophet, who connect with Islam's more pacifist teachings, coupled with Sharia law (which defers to Islamic clerics instead of legal systems of Common Law or Napoleonic Codes), Radical Islam has evolved into a doctrine that calls its subjects to obey God, obey its principles on this earth, and commit violence both in its defense and to advance its interests.

Nation states that have adopted other forms of governance have appropriate reason to be concerned with Muslim advocates within their borders. In its radical form, and indeed perhaps even among non-violent Muslims, there may be strong adherence to doctrine that the Prophet taught that competes with core and widely considered **shared** principles.

Is Sharia law more fair than Common Law or a Napoleonic Code? Fairness might compel a person to advocate for Sharia, whether or not one is a follower of Allah, if it were more fair (and in countries yet to establish the requisite education and credentialing of a modern legal community, Sharia probably is a viable and mostly fair system, if you set aside sexist and barbaric punishments that receive global publicity).

Indeed, are socialist economic organizations more fair, if not more efficient, than capitalist constructs? In an America where Bernie Sanders ran a strong candidacy for the Democratic nomination for president, these are appropriate questions for all but the most cynical. We hope that human development will move forward, not backward.

In any event, even under competing forms of government, we acknowledge that a common defense is still an appropriate component of the human experience. Thus, we turn to the common defense now… or at least, to the naval component of it.

Navies

Much has been said through history regarding Russia's need for a "warm water port." Russian annexation of Crimea in 2014 may have been driven more for it's Naval base at Sevastopol than percentage of Russian speakers in the larger territory. We examine here the rise of Russia's Navy under the mantle of the Soviet Union and the global influence Russia expects from its Black Sea fleet.

Today all of the heavy combatants of Russia's Black Sea fleet are based in Sevastopol, Crimea, along with about 70% of the rest of that fleet (29 surface vessels and 2 submarines). This armada includes a "carrier killer" Slava class guided missile cruiser ("Glory" armed with both SSN-12 anti-ship missiles along with various surface to air missiles), a Kara class anti-submarine ship equipped with various anti-submarine munitions, anti-submarine helicopters and another compliment of surface to air missiles.

The "Smetlivy" Kashin class destroyer sits in port there, along with two Krivak class missile frigates and two Nanuchka class missile corvettes. There are two Bora class guided missile hovercraft, a Matka class Missile boat and five Tarantula missile corvettes. We believe there are two B-871 Kilo class diesel-electric submarines and seven large amphibious landing ships. The fleet is completed with seven anti submarine corvettes and twelve coast patrol and minesweeping craft. (Tyler Rogoway, "Putin's Game of Battleship," www.foxtrotal-pha.jalopnik.com, March 7, 2014)

These assets are complimented with an unknown number of K-300P coastal defense missile systems, nearly a hundred shore-based helicopters of various types and a dozen medium sized transport aircraft. At the Gvardeyskoye Air base, also on Crimea, is a squadron of SU-24/M/MRs "Fencer" aircraft, armed with Kh31 and Kh-59M missiles. There is a 3000-Soldier Naval infantry brigade also stationed on Crimea. (Ibid)

So even if US or NATO vessels were able to saturate the Black Sea beyond the nine vessels per nation limit (see details of the Montreux Agreement), they would be rapidly sunk to the bottom of the salt water lake the size of California, that is the Black Sea.

The problem posed to US and NATO vessels choosing to aid Ukraine dynamics in the Black Sea also has an impact on Russia, and indeed the priority that some attribute to Sevastipol, Crimea, namely, the Bosporus Strait. Bosporus is controlled by Turkey and limits travel of Russian vessels as it does other shipping. Perhaps a more important warm water port for Russian strategic interests lies in Tartus, Syria.

The Bosporus Strait

Yet somehow Russia's interest in maintaining its port in Tartus hadn't surfaced to justify Russia's activity in Syria, nor (it seems) has Russia's intent to keep Bashar Assad in power in Syria been a factor in handling of US/European military activity supporting the Arab Spring and combating various terrorist groups in the country. Ultimately, Russian activity there has assured Syria's long-term commitment to allow Russian use of Tartus as a naval port.

Ukraine, the Bosporus Strait and Tartus, Syria

##

On May 27th, 1905, the pride of Russia's blue water navy, the 45 warships of its Baltic fleet, were steaming north through the Tsushima Strait, between the tip of what is today South Korea and southern Japan. Many of the ships in this force had traveled 18,000 nautical miles (33,000 km) with the intention of uniting with the rest of Russia's Pacific fleet and subordinating the Japanese fleet under Admiral Togo Heihachiro.

After several Naval defeats to Japan (a newly modernizing nation), the Russian Tsar had directed this "Second Pacific Squadron" to join the rest of the Russian vessels in the Pacific. Unfortunately, the Russians fired on some British fishing vessels in the North Sea (thinking they were Japanese torpedo boats), eliminating Russia's opportunity to use the British controlled Suez canal. In part due to the delay, the Japanese blockade at Port Arthur resulted in a Russian loss of the port well before the reinforcements would arrive.

The delay encouraged Russian use of the Tsushima Strait (in lieu of La Peruse or Tsugara straits), a decision correctly predicted by the Japanese Admiral, who had massed his fleet to oppose the Russians. The Russian fleet was in poor condition given the long journey and hoped to slip through the strait unnoticed. A Japanese destroyer detected lights on a Russian hospital ship, and upon investigation, received inadvertent signals from the Russian ship that there were other Russian ships nearby.

In an era where battleships were thought to rule the day, the Russian armada including 8 battleships appeared to "out gun" the Japanese fleet, which only had 4 of these massive vessels. Unfortunately for the Russians, maneuverability and the recently deployed torpedo meant that the Japanese advantage including 27 cruisers, 21 destroyers and some 37 torpedo boats overwhelmed the Russian fleet.

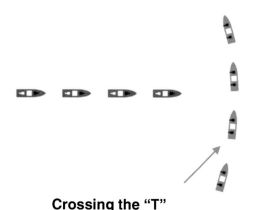

Crossing the "T"

This was the first battle to use wireless communications on both sides, but the Japanese leveraged "made in Japan" sets, while the Russians stumbled to use their own "made in Germany" sets. Due to communication, number of vessel and maneuverability advantages, the Japanese "crossed the t" twice, sinking over 21 of the Russian vessels, killing over 4,000 Russian sailors and capturing almost 6,000. Of a total of 89 ships, the Japanese lost three torpedo boats, with 117 sailors dead and 583 wounded.

Instead of breaking the blockade at Port Arthur and joining the rest of the Pacific fleet, Nicolas' navy was dealt a crushing and well publicized defeat. US President Theodore Roosevelt brokered a peace between the Tsar and the Japanese, while in Russia public discontent with the Tsar and both the serf and petty noble systems, had reached unprecedented levels.

##

Teddy Roosevelt was an appropriate dignitary to broker a peace. He entered into the United States national political scene as Secretary of the Navy (after a number of roles in New York city and state) and was well received by both Japan and Russia. Shortly after brokering the peace, Roosevelt sent the United States' "Great White Fleet" on a global tour, including visits to Japan as well as a number of European destinations. The US fleet did not include any "dreadnought" class battle-ships, but a global arms race continued, with the United States a ready participant.

Navies were not the first decisive technology advantage in human conflict and would not be the last. Ironically, the first "platform" to deliver decisive advantage in human conflict has been attributed to Ukraine: "The transformation of warfare by horses began with their domestication around 4,000 B. C. in the steppes north of the Black Sea." (Jared Diamond. Guns, Germs and Steel: The Fates of Human Societies. (W. W. Norton & Company: New York, 1999), p. 77). The Hyksos were able to dominate Egypt for a generation with the invention of the chariot, then the in-vention of the stirrup under his father enabled Alexander of Macedon to conquer the largest empire in history.

##

Clearly, Navies used to matter.

Prince Henry the Navigator began the Portuguese quest for empire in the 1400's. The Portuguese developed very heavy vessels, as well as carrack and caravel vessels to enhance trading capability. These vessels were heavy enough to sail the open ocean, small enough to navigate shallow waters, and highly maneuverable.

In the 1400 and 1500's, Portuguese interests were focused on India, and, because coastal cities there were key way stations on the route, Africa. Portugal privatized its African holdings in 1469 (selling a license to Fernao Gomes) but refused to renew the license in 1474 after the holdings had become profitable. John II of Portugal greatly expanded gold and slave trade in west Africa, then penetrated the spice trade between Europe and Asia with the help of Vasco da Gama,

A brutal character in history, da Gama represented the Portuguese king in successful naval actions against the French at Setúbal and to the Algarve, then led several exploratory armadas opening India. Follow-on armadas helped Portugal out maneuver the Venetian city state and Muslim merchants in the spice trade. Profits led to a substantial overseas empire under Manuel I of

Portugal (1469-1521), including monopolies on maritime spice trade routes and discovery of Brazil.

The empire of Spain hit its "zenith under the rule of King Philip II, who reigned from 1556 to 1598…" (Robert Sullivan, et. al. The World's Great Civilizations. Life Books: New York, 2012 pp. 92) although Spanish exploration, shipping and navies were dominant in the 1400's and continued well into the 1600s. A massing of Spanish warships were sent to strike England in 1588 resulted in an unprecedented disaster for Spain, echoing a few hundred years later at Trafalgar. The Spanish Armada was sunk or lost due to storms, while the English fleet under Nelson captured 21 French and Spanish vessels at Trafalgar.

Spanish land power insured domination of much of Europe, including the Netherlands, until the Eighty Years war, which began as a protest against Spanish taxation, ultimately involving England and triggering the attack of the Spanish Armada. Spanish colonies were maintained in the Americas until the 1800's, with descendants of the Spanish settlers still controlling much of the economy and nation states in South and Central America. Soviet ties to these colonies became a source of friction with the United States throughout the 1900's.

The Dutch became the leading maritime nation for a time, thanks to "efficient and economical ships called *fluyts*…" (Brian Lavery. The Conquest of the Ocean. DR Books: London, p.126)

Although control of the Dutch "Republic of United Provinces" fell to the English, the Portuguese, French and others, they were recognized to have one of the strongest and faster navies in the world between 1590 and 1712. Perhaps threat of foreign military power against the Dutch government prompted the formation of the East India Company, which proved a very successful experiment.

The Dutch East India company ultimately eclipsed the Portuguese in India, sending almost a million Europeans to work in "the Asia trade" on over 4,000 ships. This East India company was the first in history to issue stock, while enjoying many governmental functions such as ability to strike its' own coins and execute convicts.

Under Queen Elizabeth I, England defeated Spain, held off the French and came to control nearly a quarter of the land mass of the world. (Robert Sullivan, et. al. The World's Great Civilizations. Life Books: New York, 2012 pp. 109-110) English sea power ultimately eclipsed the Dutch East India company, but would not find the same level of commercial success in India.

Between the disaster of the Spanish Armada in 1588, and the defeat of French and Spanish navies at Trafalgar in 1805, English ship building and seamanship were recognized premier in world. For this reason (and because he could), Russian Tsar Peter the Great spent two years in England, securing trade agreements with the English crown and personally working in a shipyard to develop an understanding for the details of forming a world class navy.

The Russian Navy under the Tsars had some limited successes, but suffered from on-again, off-again funding, ultimately meeting the disastrous fate described at the beginning of this chapter. In the cloud of the Russian revolution and Soviet consolidation of power, many officers in the Russian Navy were executed for a lack of commitment to the Communist cause, undermining effectiveness and capability.

##

Josef Jughashvili was a studious and religious child who read Charles Darwin, Karl Marx and Napoleon Bonaparte as a teen, before renouncing God and dropping out of seminary. At 21 he took a job at an oil refinery on the Black Sea, observing for himself the contrast between the impoverished laborers working in horrible conditions and the company executives living in mansions and sailing their yachts. He began organizing violent protests among the workers and distributing literature from his little printing press, then was arrested for revolutionary activity and transferred to Siberia.

After a short time he was able to walk away from exile and return to Tiflis, Georgia's largest city, then earned money helping wealthy Armenians escape the Caucasus after widespread violence broke out in the power vacuum of the Tsar's humiliating defeat to the Japanese. There were pogroms against the Jewish, Muslims slaughtering Christians and Christians slaughtering Muslims. Josef's pamphlets began to emphasize the importance of abandoning ethnic violence in favor of a unified people's struggle.

At this time, Josef began traveling to attend Bolshevik conferences at other cities in Europe (in Finland and Sweden), meeting Vladimir Illych Lenin in Stockholm in 1905. Josef was mesmerized and began robbing banks to fund the Bolshevik operation. Sometime between the years of 1910 and 1912, Josef began using the name Stalin in his writings.

Josef Stalin wasn't drafted to serve in the Tsar's army for World War I because one of his arms was shorter than the other. Instead, he went to St Petersburg, where he was able to seize control of Pravda, a Revolutionary paper, just in time for the successful Russian Revolution of 1917. He endorsed Kerensky's provisional government, then the Bolsheviks. Shortly after endorsing them, Stalin was elected to the Bolshevik Central Committee.

Russian revolutionaries broke into two parties after the overthrow of the Tsar, White and Red, with the Reds including Lenin, Stalin, Trotsky and several others in its leading polit-buro. After playing an active role in "disciplining" deserters, former Tsarist officers and entire uncooperative villages, Stalin assumed a more military role in attacks to broaden Soviet control, in Poland and ultimately Georgia. After his successes in Georgia, Stalin was appointed General Secretary in 1922. And so it was that Stalin became the prime intermediary between Lenin and the rest of the leadership when Lenin, the Bolshevik thought leader and undisputed chief, succumbed to two strokes that year.

The Soviet navy had been established as the "Workers and Peasants Red Fleet" in 1918, although it had been decimated through "Red Terror" killings of officers and sailor desertions. The Soviet's Labour and Defense Council of 1926 established a Naval Shipbuilding program with plans to build twelve submarines in the Baltic shipyard. According to Wikipedia, "…there re-mained [in the Baltic Sea] three much-neglected battleships, two cruisers, some ten destroyers, and a few submarines [while in] the Black Sea Fleet [there] existed some thirty minor-waterways combat flotillas."

In 1932 and 1933, the Pacific and Northern fleets respectively, were to be built around Soviet Soyuz (also known as Stalin's Republics) class battleships, but construction of the first four ships stalled because of serious construction flaws, then prevented due to the invasion of the Nazi's in June 1941. Although these efforts were unsuccessful in producing ships for the war, they built a core of expertise that resulted in the construction of a significant naval presence after World War II.

Paul Gregory sketches the intrigue of the Stalin politburo in his book, Behind the Facade of Stalin's Command Economy: Evidence from the Soviet State and Party Archives (Hoover Institute Press: Stanford, 2001), although he seems to miss the (somewhat justified) paranoia fueling the passion of the new Soviet State for building a strong military. In spite of well-known purges, the Soviet Union was able to build capability across its Armed Forces, such that with United States assistance of trucks and other material, the Red Army held Nazi Germany at St Petersburg, then pushed the Germans back to the very border of Western Europe before the truce in 1945.

The Naval Forces in the Far East were created in April of 1932, renamed the Pacific Fleet in 1935, and remained on perpetual alert for the duration of World War II. The fleet had surface, submarine and torpedo boat subdivisions as well as patrol

boat and airborne units. According to Wikipedia, the force included "two cruisers, one destroyer leader, ten destroyers, two
torpedo boats, 19 patrol boats, 78 submarines, ten minelayers,
52 minesweepers, 49 "MO" anti-submarine boats (MO stands for
Малый Охотник, or "little hunter"), 204 motor torpedo boats and
1459 war planes."

The Soviet Union remained neutral with respect to Japan,
until 1945, when the fleet participated in the removal of the
Empire of Japan from North Korea, South Sakhalin and the Kuril
Islands. Plans to improve the Navy were aggressive after the
war (chart from Paul Gregory, Behind the Facade of Stalin's Command Economy) but Kuznetsov, Naval Commander in Chief, was em-
barrassed in budget conflicts by General Voroshilov, who rose to
be Chairman of the Presidium of the USSR.

DEFENSE PLANS, FIFTH FIVE-YEAR PLAN: MILITARY EQUIPMENT SUPPLY FOR 1951–1955

Draft of Jan. 23, 1950, Min. Rub. Prices 1950

	1950 (results)	1951	1952	1953	1954	1955	Total
Aviation	8750	13600	16000	18000	19500	20500	87600
Weapons	2380	3780	5210	6900	8510	9280	33680
Navy (ship construction)	5340	6230	7930	9230	10860	12400	46650
Ammunition	2550	4640	6400	7600	9600	10500	38740
Armored technics	1110	2120	3710	5190	6760	7910	25690
Military-technical equipment	2270	4020	4900	5980	7220	8340	30460
—Radiolocation technics	1100						
Total	24120	36940	47200	56800	66860	74100	281900

Stalin's last five year plan was revealed in 1952 during the Soviet Union's Nineteenth Party Congress. In his book, Khruschev Remembers, Stalin's successor states that the plan "was the worst Five-Year Plan ever accepted by a Party Congress… the plan was an impossible one, [and] we had no choice but to introduce some amendments." (Nikita Khrushchev, Khrushchev Remembers, p. 278). That said, the Russian navy expanded quite aggressively through the 1950's.

Upon Stalin's death in 1953, Nikita Khruschev was able to undermine rivals, ultimately attaining roles as First Secretary of the Communist Party and Premier (Chairman of the Council of Ministers). Although he had been born on Kursk, Russia, Nikita's family moved to the Donbass region of Ukraine, where his father found work and young Nikita learned metal working skills. Metal working kept Khruschev out of the Tsar's Army in World War I and positioned him well for election to the worker's council in Rucherkovo, where he rapidly became chairman.

Khruschev joined the Bolsheviks in 1918, serving through the Revolution in the Red Army as political commissar. Unlike most Western Armies, the Soviet Armed Forces had political appointees who observed commanders and staff, insuring diligence, expertise and loyalty to Communist Party values. This experience served as a foundation for Khrushchev's role as political

commissar at higher levels during World War II, although Nikita's political ascendence was probably due more to his relationship with Lazar Kaganovich, who became party head in Ukraine
in 1925.

After assignments in Kharkov and Kiev, Khrushchev traveled
to Moscow to study in the Industrial Academy, where he became
party secretary, before moving to party roles in the Bauman district where the Academy was located, and then in Moscow city,
where his mentor Kaganovich had been appointed to lead the party
organization. Khruschev received the Order of Lenin for his
work on the Moscow Metro, then became First Secretary of the
Moscow Regional Committee. In 1937, Stalin sent him to head the
Communist Party in Ukraine. Khrushchev returned to Moscow in
1949, assuming responsibility for the USSR in 1953 (as mentioned
above).

Babiracki explained that Stalin's death in 1953 led to several changes in how the Soviet leadership governed both domesti-
cally and internationally. For example, the Soviet security police's power was reduced, discrediting earlier methods of rule.
In Poland's case, the recall of the notoriously heavy-handed Soviet ambassador, Georgii Popov, in March of 1954 constituted one
of the most obvious signs of improvement in Soviet-Polish relations. The era of "collective leadership," in addition to
Khrushchev's ascendance to power, offered new possibilities for

reciprocal cultural relations and more flexible Soviet approach.
(Amy Liedy. "Soviet Soft Power and the Polish Thaw, 1943-57,"
Kennan Institute, Wilson Center. Nov 12, 2011 see web citation
below).

Other aspects of the "Thaw" in the USSR and Poland, however, further complicated the work of Soviet international out-
reach institutions, revealing the limitations of Soviet soft
power and of the Kremlin's capacity to maintain empire via non-
coercive means. The new Soviet "hands off" approach to East European affairs, according to Babiracki, meant that a number of
institutions that hitherto intervened in the cultural affairs of
the Soviet Union's East European satellites were suddenly de-
prived of Moscow's support.

Babiracki asserts that many Soviet officials working for
these organizations had good ideas about how to run them more
effectively, and thus did not require heavy-handed Moscow intervention. For instance, the Soviet Information Bureau, which had
been pressuring East European newspaper editors to publish Soviet articles, faced budget and staffing cuts. Freedom, the Soviet army's newspaper for the Polish population, was shut down
at the end of 1954. (https://www.wilsoncenter.org/publica-
tion/soviet-soft-power-and-the-polish-thaw-1943-
57#sthash.ixN39KTT.dpuf)

The Soviets put down a revolt in Georgia, along with subsequent revolutions in Hungary and Poland.

Perhaps Khruschev's most important decision regarding the navy was appointing Sergey Gorshkov as its commander in chief, in 1956. Gorshkov had joined the Soviet Navy in 1927, retiring after Brezhnev's tenure, in 1985. Upon his appointment to the Naval Commander in Chief role, Gorshkov immediately set about communicating to Khruschev and the rest of the Communist Party that there was a need for a strong Navy. He claimed Russian land power doctrine was Imperialist Propaganda designed to keep the Soviets from dominating the seas, observing that the Soviet Union had the world's longest maritime frontier. (Chipman, p. 1)

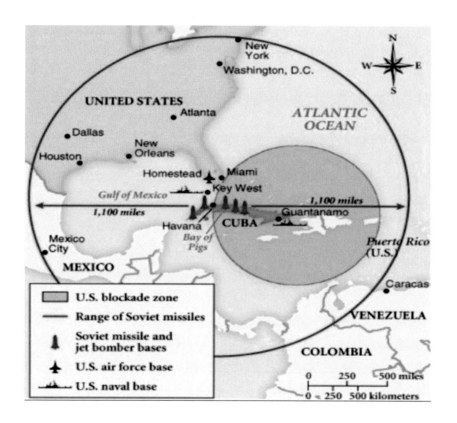

Then in 1962, Khruschev persuaded Fidel Castro to accept
medium range nuclear missiles. The flotilla that Khrushchev
dispatched with the missiles aboard led to the Cuban Missile
Crisis in 1962, where the US Naval blockade successfully prevented delivery.

Gorshkov's prescient recommendations about increasing Navy
strength before the Cuban Missile Crisis assured his credibility, and enabled improvements to the Soviet Navy in response to
NATO capabilities as well. NATO in turn was driven by events
such as the 1948 Communist overthrow of the the Czech Republic,
Soviet Berlin blockade and detonation of an atomic bomb in 1949.

##

The North Atlantic Treaty Organization was founded in 1949
to address collective security against the USSR, as well as to
eliminate any revival of Nationalist militarism in Europe
through a strong American presence on that continent. Article 5
of the NATO charter asserted that any attack on one NATO member
constituted an attack on all members.

Greece and Turkey joined NATO in 1952, while West Germany
joined during the same year (1955) that the Warsaw Pact was for-
malized. The Soviets seized control of Hungary and shocked the

west with the Sputnik satellite program in 1956. France withdrew from NATO in 1966, inspiring relocation of SHAPE headquarters to Belgium and NATO headquarters to Brussels, both in 1967.

Although some observe that the Soviet Union stagnated in-
ternally during his tenure, the global influence of the Union
grew dramatically during the 18 years of Leonid Brezhnev leadership, at least in part due to the expansion of conventional
forces (including the navy). Like Khruschev, Brezhnev was born
in Russia but spent his early career in Ukraine. Brezhnev at-
tended Dniprodzerzhynsk Metallurgical Technicum in Ukraine, becoming a metallurgical engineer in the iron and steel industry.
He joined Komsomol in 1923, and in 1929 became an active member
of the CPSU.

Brezhnev was drafted into the Red Army during World War II,
leaving the service in 1948 at the rank of Major General. Wikipedia observes:

> A significant increase in military expenditure, which by
> the time of Brezhnev's death stood at approximately 12.5%
> of the country's GNP, and an aging and ineffective
> leadership set the stage for a dwindling GNP compared to
> Western nations. While at the helm of the USSR, Brezhnev
> pushed for détente between the Eastern and Western
> countries. At the same time he presided over the Warsaw
> Pact invasion of Czechoslovakia to stop the Prague Spring,
> and his last major decision in power was to send the Soviet
> Military to Afghanistan in an attempt to save [it in] a war
> against the mujahideen.

With the rise of Leonid Brezhnev as General Secretary, Gorshkov began to elaborate on Soviet Naval policies addressing three key challenges facing a Soviet blue water navy: 1) ice; 2) chokepoints; and 3) distance. Gorshkov developed one of the world's most formidable ice breaker fleets. To address choke points and distance, "during the 1960s [Soviet deployments extended] Baltic, Northern, and Black Sea fleets …<into> spheres of influence out of their traditional deployment areas."

In addition, according to Chipman, the Soviet Black Sea Fleet began deploying into the eastern Mediterranean while the Northern Fleet journeyed into the mid-Atlantic. By the early 1970s, the Soviets were deploying to the Cuban and South African areas and into the Indian Ocean. These deployments included "sea presence," or the peaceful use of naval ships in foreign areas, "sea control," (antisubmarine warfare and interdiction), "power projection" (amphibious warfare capability) and "deterrence," (submarine ballistic missile capability). (Chipman, p. 1-2).

Thus, largely thanks to Gorshkov, before the end of Brezhnev's tenure in 1982, the Pacific fleet alone had "150,000 men and 800 ships operating between Madagascar and California…. expected to carry out… sea and air probes [against the American fleet] along the USSR's Far Eastern periphery from bases in

South Korea, Japan, Hawaii and Alaska." (Naval Postgrad School, The Russian Navy… p.77).

Number of Warships Delivered Each Year Since the End of World War II

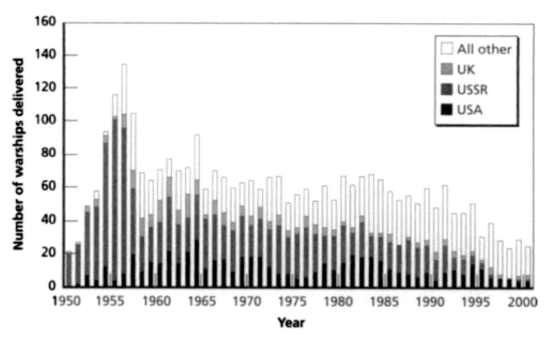

RAND MG236-2.1

Two days after the death of Leonid Brezhnev, Yuri Andropov was appointed General Secretary of the Communist Party of the USSR, becoming Premier less than a year later. Andropov was born in the Stavropol region (Russia in June 1914) and, like Khruschev, became a full-time party official during his university years. During World War II, he worked as a partisan in Finland. In 1947, he was elected Second Secretary of the Central Committee of the Communist Party of the Karelo-Finnish SSR.

Andropov was Premier when Ronald Reagan delivered the "evil empire" speech, urging his audience to reject the politically growing movement for a unilateral nuclear freeze and challenging the American people and government to hold the Soviet Union accountable. The "Star Wars" missile defense system was also announced, inspiring Andropov's accusation that the United States was preparing a first strike attack, hoping to win a nuclear war. His short stint as Premier included conversations seeking to diffuse the threat of nuclear war.

Yuri Andropov appointed Vladimir Chernavin Commander in Chief of the Soviet Navy in 1985. Chernavin remained responsible for the Commonwealth of Independent States Navy, and subsequently for the Russian Federation after the CIS dissolved. Boris Yeltsin appointed Feliks Gromov to the post after Chernavin retired in 1992.

Chernavin was born in Ukraine and had joined the Navy before the end of World War II, but saw no action since he remained in Naval school until 1951. He took command of a November-class submarine in 1959, and commanded the submarine flotillas of the Northern Fleet after a successful division command (and graduating from both Naval and General Staff Academies). He served as overall Commander of the Northern Fleet from 1977 to 1981, then was deputy to Gorshkov until his predecessor's retirement in 1985.

After three elderly leaders died in quick succession (www.bbc.co.uk) Mikhail Gorbachev was appointed General Secretary. Concerned with the stalled Soviet economy and the large budgets that the military required, Gorbachev held various nuclear summits and scaled back investment in the Navy.

Although political forces quickly spun beyond what Mikhael Gorbachev was able to control, decisions under Boris Yeltsin (advised by a young recently separated KGB lieutenant colonel named Vladimir Putin) were designed to build a viable, internationally competitive economy.

Because the Russian economy was languishing through the 1990's, the Russian Navy was chronically underfunded. In April 2001 Russia Navy Commander-in-Chief, Adm Vladimir Kuroyedov stated that the Navy should consist of 12-15 strategic missile submarines, 50 nuclear-powered attack submarines and 35 diesel submarines, along with about 70 ocean-going surface combatants. but conceded to achieve these goals the Navy would need to receive at least 25% of the Russian defense budget, double the allocation available (about 12%). ("Russian Navy - Fleet Modernization 2000's" GlobalSecurity.org)

Budgetary pressure forced the commander of the Russian Navy to admit in early 2003 that the navy budget would be slashed by one-fifth or about 12 percent of requested funding. (Ibid.)

Oil profits changed all this after 2005. Navy Commander-in-Chief Vladimir Kuroyedov began claiming that the surface combatant force would not be downsized until 2020, thanks to funded repairs and general maintenance. Putin was realizing that status of a great power only remains if the nation can maintain world class navy, which is impossible without a "modern, well-balanced fleet." (Ibid.)

The older small surface vessels were discarded first, replaced with "the corvette – a new multifunctional littoral combat ship, which combines qualities of anti-submarine ships and missile carriers." The Russian Navy placed orders for the Scorpion Project 1230.0 475-ton fast patrol craft and the Project 2038.0 1800-ton Steregushchy class corvette, with delivery due in 2003-2005. At the time, Russia hoped to build 12 of the fast patrol craft and 10 Project 2038.0 corvettes. (Ibid.)

Russian plans for a multifunctional frigate and an oceangoing torpedo boat destroyer were also announced in the early 2000's, with mass production of these vessels expected a decade after that. (Ibid.)

As of the end of 2003 the Russian navy consisted of 300 ships, 400 aircraft and helicopters, 150,000 personnel and 120,000 employees. After languishing at 90/10 through much of the 1990's, the ratio between maintaining the fleet and new building had been raised to 60/40. (Ibid.)

New building expanded to produce several dozen surface ships and submarines, "including five Project 955 Borey nuclear-powered strategic ballistic missile submarines equipped with new Bulava-30 ballistic missiles, two Project 885 Yasen nuclear-powered multipurpose submarines, six Project 677 Lada diesel-electric submarines, three Project 22350 multipurpose frigates and five Project 20380 corvettes." (Ibid.)

"As of mid-2006 there were about 50 large surface ships in the Russian naval fleet. This included one aircraft carrier, four Project 1144 and 1164 missile cruisers (with two more Project 1144 cruisers laid up), ten Project 956 destroyers, 12 large antisubmarine ships and 25 large amphibious ships." Some of these vessels were under repair or awaiting major overhauls and thus were not combat ready. (Ibid.)

At the same time, there were 45 nuclear submarines and 20 diesel submarines in the Russian fleet. Although the fleet includes three Project 941 ballistic missile submarines, the Dmitry Donskoi was a test pad for the Bulava missile, the Severstal was under renovation, and the Arkhangelsk had no missiles. The main nuclear deterrent were the six Project 667BDRM missile submarines [one of which is under renovation], and six Project 667BDR vessels. Of the nine Project 959A submarines with anti-ship missiles, two were under renovation. And of the 21 Projects 971, 945 and 671RTMK nuclear torpedo submarines, at least six were under repair/renovation. Of the 20 Project 636, 877 and 641B diesel submarines, only 12 were actually combat-ready. By 2010 it seemed the best-case scenario would be five or six Project 667BDRM ballistic missile submarines and one or two new Project 955 submarines available at any one time, with the total number of submarines reduced to 35 or 40. (Ibid.)

In September 2005 President Putin replaced the Head Commander of the Russian Navy, Vladimir Kuroedov, with Vladimir Masorin. Putin and Minister of Defense Sergei Ivanov proceeded to revamp Russia's military policy thanks to significant economic growth and the earlier mentioned influx of cash from oil and natural gas exports. The giant "State Armaments Program" was approved for the sum of 4.9 trillion rubles, of which 25% was allocated toward the production of new ships. The development of the naval program had achieved parity with the strategic nuclear forces. (Ibid.)

Today Russia divides its Naval forces into five fleets: The Northern, Baltic, Black Sea, Caspian, and Pacific, although the navy may still suffer from relative low readiness levels, with most units remaining close to home port. The Pacific and Northern Fleets are considered the two most powerful Russian naval forces. ("Russian Naval Forces," www.geographic.org)

Pacific Fleet headquarters is in Vladivostok, with additional home ports in Petropavlovsk-Kamchatskiy, Magadan, and Sovetskaya Gavan. The Pacific Fleet includes eighteen nuclear submarines that are operationally subordinate to the Ministry of Defense and based at Pavlovsk and Rybachiy. The blue-water striking power of the Pacific Fleet lies in thirty-four nonnuclear submarines and forty-nine principal surface combatants. (Ibid)

The Northern Fleet is headquartered at Severomorsk, at the top of the Kola Peninsula near Murmansk, with additional home ports at Kola, Motovskiy, Gremikha, and Ura Guba. The mission of the Northern Fleet is to defend Russia's far northwestern Arctic region surrounding the Kola Peninsula. The fleet provides home ports for thirty-seven nuclear submarines, twenty-two other submarines, forty-seven principal surface combatants, and ten coastal and smaller ships. The naval aviation contingent includes a complement of twenty Su-39 fixed-wing aircraft and ten antisubmarine warfare helicopters on board the *Admiral Kuznetsov*, which heads the air defense of the Barents Sea. Shore-based naval aviation includes 200 combat aircraft and sixty-four helicopters. The Northern Fleet has two naval infantry brigades, one coastal defense regiment, and an air defense missile regiment. (Ibid)

The Baltic Fleet is headquartered in Kaliningrad, where it is defended by a naval infantry brigade. From this rather exposed location, the fleet controls naval bases at Kronshtadt and Baltiysk. Operational forces include nine submarines, twenty-three principal surface combatants, and approximately sixty-five smaller vessels. The air arm of the Baltic Fleet includes five regiments of combat aircraft and a number of other fixed-wing aircraft and helicopters. (Ibid)

Headquartered at Sevastopol, with an additional home port in Odessa, the Black Sea Fleet became an object of contention between Russia and Ukraine when the latter republic achieved independence after the dissolution of the Soviet Union. Although Ukraine has no use for a blue-water navy and cannot afford to maintain one, it had been reluctant to surrender its share of the fleet, both of whose home ports were in Ukraine (before Putin's recent annexation of Crimea). A long international squabble ended temporarily when a June 1995 summit meeting arrived at a formula for disposition of the Black Sea Fleet's assets: the ships of the fleet were to be divided equally between the two nations, but Russia would ultimately buy back approximately 60 percent of Ukraine's share. The Russian portion of the Black Sea Fleet continued to be based in Sevastopol, with separate Russian and Ukrainian ports designated on the coast. All ships were to be under dual command, placed under Ukrainian command in 1998, until being seized by Russia in 2014. (Ibid)

The Black Sea Fleet comprises fourteen submarines, thirty-one capital ships of the line, and forty-one coastal ships. The *Moskva*, Russia's first seagoing aircraft cruiser, is assigned to the Black Sea Fleet. It is an antisubmarine warfare helicopter carrier with a complement of eighteen KA-25 helicopters. The land component of the Black Sea Fleet comprises one naval infantry brigade, a coastal defense division, and a surface-to-air missile (SAM) regiment…. The naval aviation component of the fleet includes an inventory of nearly 8,000 aircraft of all types. Its strike power is concentrated in a bomber regiment and a mixed fighter and ground-attack regiment. (Ibid)

The Caspian Flotilla is a small force for coastal defense and waterway patrol including two frigates, twelve patrol boats, and about fifty other small craft based in Astrakhan. Command and equipment are shared with Azerbaijan and Kazakstan. (Ibid)

The air power of the Pacific Fleet consists of the 250 combat aircraft and helicopters of the Pacific Fleet Air Force. The two bomber regiments stationed at Alekseyevka are its most powerful weapon systems. Each regiment consists of thirty supersonic Tu-26 Backfire aircraft. In addition to these land-based aircraft, the Pacific Fleet controls one naval infantry division and a coastal defense division. (Ibid)

In addition to the infantry division subordinate to the Pacific Fleet described earlier, the Russian Navy has four naval infantry brigades--one in the Baltic Fleet, one in the Black Sea Fleet, and two in the Northern Fleet. The coastal defense forces are a combination of infantry regiments, brigades, and divisions with air defense missile regiments. Amphibious landings are a low priority; Russia's thirteen amphibious ships have a capacity to carry 2,500 marines and 100 tanks. ("Russian Naval Forces," www.geographic.org)

Although Putin hopes recent and projected investments will make the Russian the second largest navy in the world by 2020-2025, "Russian officials denied this large navy represented any intentions of getting into a naval arms race with the United States." ("Russian Navy - Fleet Modernization 2000's" GlobalSecurity.org)

Other investment plans include "technologically innovative and newly built strategic nuclear-powered submarines, and a force of six aircraft carriers. The six carriers would be divided into two powerful strike groups, one in the Pacific and one in the Atlantic. Each would have a total of three carriers at its disposal: one carrier for active operations; one on call and ready to be deployed at a moments notice; with the third un-

Mr Putin celebrated Victory Day last year with a military parade in Sevastopol

dergoing maintenance and repairs." (Ibid)

Investments included a dock, capable of building gas carriers - ships to transport Russian liquefied natural gas to Western partners, as well as aircraft carriers. Recent investments in submarines included repairs/upgrades to four boats, including the two Project 667 BDRM boats. Upgrades include a new sonar systems, new fire fighting systems, nuclear reactor protection devices, and the RSM-54 Sineva strategic missile system. Unlike its predecessor, the Skif, Sineva missiles carry 10 independently targetable re-entry vehicles instead of four. The new missile also has a longer range and a modern control system. (Ibid)

Recent pressure on the Russian economy compels more careful expenditures moving forward. Although the world appears significantly more peaceful (on land and in the sea) than in 1941 when a shell exchange resulting in the sinking of Great Britain's HMS Hood and (a few days later) the attack on (and ultimate scuttling of) Germany's Bismarck battleship by torpedo fighter-bombers, naval strategists still suggest that a great power can ill afford to miss a significant technology upgrade. The salient question: what technology upgrade is most critical at any juncture?

Naval strategies still include supplementing nuclear deterrence and protecting sea lanes, but because of the capabilities and ranges of low cost ant-ship missiles, and other methods available for sinking them, technologies for finding and targeting vessels, protecting or cloaking vessels from detection in the first place, are a huge component of naval development in the modern world.

In the era of the new United States space force, we must include at least a brief conversation about geopositioning infrastructure. Specialized satellite constellations help land, naval and air forces navigate more precisely, locate threatening equipment or other forces with precision, and, when deemed necessary, deploy munitions to remove a threat. Capabilities to place space-based geopositioning equipment are non-trivial, even after sophisticated systems are designed and built. Once in place and operational, forces must protect the safety of a device while layered protections are necessary to insure the system isn't vulnerable to complete electronic disablement or even a minor precision adjustment which might move a weapon system impact from a menacing piece of military equipment to a school or hospital.

In the latest United States Quadrenial Defense Review, the Defense Department has acknowledged a reemergence of "great power" concerns. "Pivot to the Pacific" prioritization acknowledges the surging threat emanating from China. After recognition of the Communist Chinese under Richard Nixon, it took decades for Western commercial entities to build the capability in China to fully enable capitalizing on rock bottom labor costs available there. Unfortunately, China built capabilities well beyond the commercial, with severe consequences given China's consistent aversion to Western values of freedom—of speech, of religion, of assembly—and democracy.

While Russia, Europe and the United States have long had geospatial positioning technologies available for non-military and military application (with dramatic benefits to respective navies), China's participation in Europe's Galileo geopositioning project secured China's ability to deploy multiple generations of it's own "BeiDou" navigation systems.

In any event, there are two realities associated with Navies: first, they require substantial petrol for operation; and second, at least for the much of the rest of the world, Navies protecting sea lanes are critical to delivering petrol products which fuel the world's economy. Thus, we turn to a more careful examination of petrol, as we examine US policy with regards to Russia and Ukraine.

USS Zumwalt

Petrol

Crude oil prices were $86 bbl in December, 1990. At their highest in 1979, they were $117.18 bbl. In January of the year this book was first published (2016), prices were $28 bbl (www.inflationdata.com), while price per barrel rose above $50 in January 2021, after recently inaugurated President Biden's early decision to end fracking for oil on US public land. Oil is a key policy driver for net producers of the commodity… and for net consumers.

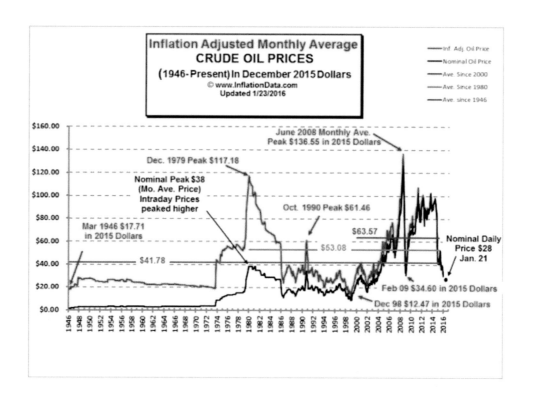

Russia is a net producer. Ukraine, and Western Europe, are net consumers. The Mideast is one of the largest net producers, but many net producers have emerged in the years since the First Gulf War (including the United States). As of February 2021, the Energy Industry Association projects that the US will return to being a net petroleum importer in 2021 and 2022. (www.eia.gov/petroleum/weekly/).

Webster defines petrol as "gasoline," a substance derived from petroleum for powering internal combustion engines (cars, trucks, etc.). The chapter title is more expansive, however, generally referring to any flammable hydrocarbon, including natural gas ("a colorless, highly flammable mixture of mostly methane and ethane").

This chapter will outline projections for Ukraine deep water reserves in the Black Sea (off the coast of Crimea) and provide a brief overview of the impact of anti-carbon protests in Europe specifically and globally in general.

In light of Hunter Biden's involvement with a Ukrainian natural gas firm and the impeachment proceedings against Donald Trump due to a call to Ukraine about Biden's dealings, this chapter will also address corruption in government and business. Admittedly the rumblings of corruption in Ukraine oil and gas industry isn't a uniquely American phenomenon. Ukraine presidential candidate Iulia Timoshenko was implicated and even jailed for a time on corruption charges before European Union pressures caused her release.

Europe has been involved with politics between Russia and Ukraine since before the natural gas scandals, although certainly those events irrevocably intertwined the Union with the Russia/Ukraine conflict. Europe is investing in Ukrainian Democracy with formal election observers and political visibility. The Union helped install a system to prevent voter fraud and has worked to have hackers threatening Ukraine voting infrastructure arrested. Indeed, Europe has a substantial stake in reducing the corruption that appears manifest in Ukraine, corruption that is still evident at the writing of this book.

We have already seen evidence of corruption associated with oil and gas. American George Soros (in October 2014) named Ukraine's Naftohaz to be "a black hole in the budget and a major source of corruption" and called for a radical reform of the company, which could "totally eliminate Ukraine's dependence on Russia for gas."

In addition, in February of 2016, Aivaras Abromavicius resigned from his post as Economic Development Minister in Ukraine, because he claimed various officials, including Petro Poroshenko were attempting inappropriate influence. Poroshenko isn't the only official so accused: "Prosecutor General Viktor

Shokin, for example, stepped down on Poroshenko's advice in February, after accusations from anti-corruption organizations, MPs and protesters that he was at best ineffective at combating corruption and at worst corrupt himself." (Kateryna Kruk, "Kiev's Leaders Have Let Us Down," Newsweek, 3/8/2016).

When the Soviet Union dissolved in 1991, Russia's oil production had been stalled for years. The Soviet Union's Ministry of Oil and Gas had been renamed Rosneftgaz, then renamed simply Rosneft. This organization was subsequently split into ten integrated companies. "Ownership of some of Russia's most valuable resources was auctioned off by oligarch-owned banks... Although they were supposedly acting on behalf of the state, the bank auctioneers rigged the process-and in almost every case ended up as the successful bidders." (Marshall Goldman, "Putin and the Oligarchs," November/December 2004, published for the Council for Foreign Relations).

Of course, oil and gas interests in Russia were established before the communists. According to Wikipedia, Russia contains over 30 percent of the world's natural resources, estimated to be worth $75.7 trillion, making it the most resource rich country in the world.

##

For thousands of years, humans used fire and various wood products to address cooking, heating and light after dark. Whale oil saw a heyday for several hundred years (16th through 19th Centuries) and coal gas was popular in cities, with various petroleum products slowly gaining adoption as methods for obtaining, refining and delivering these products were improved. Abraham Gesner (Canadian) and James Young (Scotch) independently developed processes for producing kerosene (or paraffin, as it was called in UK and other British speaking territories) and established commercial relationships with lighting companies after obtaining US patents for producing the fuel from coal.

Samuel Martin Kier (American) and Ignacy Lukasiewicz (a Pole with strong European business for both refining the fuel and manufacturing lamps to burn it) developed methods for producing kerosene from petroleum. John D. Rockefeller founded Standard Oil in 1870, and consolidated production, refining and delivery of kerosene (producing multiple different petroleum derivatives), ultimately dominating US and even global markets with aggressive production economies of scale and monopolistic transportation pricing. Standard Oil was broken up by the US Supreme Court for monopolistic practices in 1911.

Rockefeller continued to remain active in the global petroleum industry, reportedly knocking the Swedish Nobel brothers from very lucrative Azerbaijan oil fields via overthrow of the Tsar (who had fashioned agreements with the Nobels). Although tracing dollar flows at this stage is a challenge for historians, Stalin may have received funding for various revolutionary activities from Rockefeller representatives interested in the Azerbaijani oil fields. The Communist revolution spun out of control and Rockefeller interests did not ultimately obtain control or even sourcing of petroleum from Azerbaijan (although the Nobels were forced out of the oil business).

After the fall of the Tsar, the Soviet oil industry was established and (according to the CIA) saw Soviet oil consumption increase at roughly a 7% per year rate and oil production increase at roughly an 8% per year (1960 to 1975). During that time the CIA estimates that the Soviet Union had a roughly 6% rate of economic growth.

The global petroleum and gas industry became characterized by aggressive interaction on commodities financial markets and ultimately a number of large multinational corporations responsible for exploration, extraction, refining and marketing of oil and gas products. Several of these corporations founded the Organization of Petroleum Exporting Countries in 1960, although control of OPEC rapidly shifted to the governments where the largest oil fields were located. Soviet Union involvement with

OPEC included a tight relationship with socialist Baath regimes in Syria and Iraq.

As the industry evolved, "...the level of investment in new and developmental drilling <in Russia> according to the CIA was increasing in the late 1970's and early 1980's. Gustafson says the number of exploration wells completed increased by 6.5% from 1965 to 1975, and capital spending on oil and gas exploration increased by 27% from 1980 to 1985 with even greater increases in investment in other oil and gas infrastructure needs." (Ibid)

In spite of this exploration, from 1975 to 1980, the Soviet Union had a much lower 4% per year increase in use of oil and only a 3.5% increase in yearly production. Soviet economic growth overall fell to 2.6% during that period. Then from 1980 to 1985, Soviet oil consumption was flat, with production suffering a slight decline. Finally, from 1988 to 1992, Soviet and post Soviet oil production collapsed, as did consumption. At that time both Eastern Europe and the Former Soviet Union went into severe economic decline. (IBID)

In response to this decline, Soviet leadership began a rapid privatization process of the oil and gas industries, creating firms such as Yukos and TNK, and remarkable wealth, for oligarchs like Mikhail Khodorkovsky and Mikhail Fridman.

Other industry participants, like Vagit Alekperov, originally an Azerbaijani, were educated on the petroleum technology and economics, earning distinction working in the industry. Alekperov was a deputy minister of the Oil and Gas Industry of the Soviet Union at the time of privatization and today runs LU-Koil. Alekperov is worth $12.3B, reportedly the eighth richest person in Russia.

In his book, <u>Once</u> <u>Upon</u> <u>a</u> <u>Time</u> <u>in</u> <u>Russia</u>, chronicling the rise of Russia's oligarchs, Ben Mezrich describes a July 2000 meeting in which some of the world's wealthiest men were told (by Vladimir Putin, shortly after he won election), "You can keep what you have. Business is important. Industry is important. But from here on our <sic> you are simply businessmen—and only businessmen." (<u>Once</u>, Atria Books: New York, 2015, p6)

Mikhail Khodorkovsky, one time owner of Yukos and one time richest man in Russia, was the first oligarch to fall victim to Putin's threat. He was arrested in October 2003, losing much of his wealth to collapse of Yukos share prices and tax charges. Ultimately, Putin pardoned Khodorkovsky (in 2013) and allowed the man to leave the country, where he lives on his much reduced $100 or $200M fortune, promoting a number of Russian reforms.

Khodorkovsky's experience might be contrasted with that of Mikhail Osipov, who graduated from the Grozny Oil Institute in 1983 and attained executive status in the 2000's, ultimately assuming chairmanship of Slavneft several years ago. Slavneft is a Joint-Stock Oil and Gas Company that conducts exploration, development, production, refining and sale of oil throughout Russia.

After obtaining physics and mathematics degrees in Lviv, Ukraine, Mikhail Fridman founded the Alpha Group with some friends, compiling a fortune trading imports/exports and delivering a number of less glamorous services. Fridman owns L1 Energy, with $25B in assets that profited from a TNK-BP sale and also owns Vimpelcom, Turkcell and other investments. According to Forbes, Friedman is the second wealthiest Russian at this writing.

Viktor Chernomyrdin was the longest serving Prime Minister of Russia (serving from 1992 to 1998). He transformed the Soviet Ministry of Gas into Gazprom and served as its first chairman, although unlike a long list of Russian oligarchs, he doesn't appear to have acquired a fortune as a result. Chernomyrdin died in November 2010 after a long illness.

In June 2000, when Vladimir Putin became the President of Russia, he fired Chernomyrdin from his position as the Chairman of the Gazprom board, replacing him (and his deputy Vyakhirev) with Dmitry Medvedev and Alexai Miller (Putin confidants from Saint Petersburg). Hermitage Capital Management CEO William Browder and former Russian finance Minister Boris Fyodorov also assisted Putin with this reorganization.

Leadership at western firms are inevitably growth driven, but large firms, like Exxon, find it increasingly challenging to find meaningful growth. Under the newly privatized model, Russian oil production appeared to provide an opportunity to Exxon for growth and addressing world demand. Specifically, Tom Bower asserts that satisfying world demand required increasing Russian oil production from "10 million barrels a day to 12 million. Bower asserts that such an increase would hinge on Khodorkovsky's modernization of Yukos," which in turn would only be possible with innovation and efficiencies that an Exxon merger might deliver. (Oil: Money, Politics and Power in the 21st Century. Grand Central Publishing: New York, 2009, p.13).

Although the acquisition and subsequent modernization appeared on track and achievable, the negotiations between Yukos and Exxon spooked Vladimir Putin. Khodorkovsky was arrested, the merger was cancelled and Russia's oil production slipped. This gambit would allow Putin to unilaterally choose to satisfy "all Europe's energy requirements," (IBID) or not.

Oil and Gas have historically been a key component of a viable, internationally competitive economy, and Ukraine was expected to play a substantial role in that vital post-Soviet economy. The Soviet Union resolved to build what became the largest pipeline network in the world, Druzhba, in 1958, at the 10th session of the Council for Mutual Economic Assistance held in Prague. The first part of the pipeline was put in operation in 1964, then expanded in the 1970's. For much of the period, the Druzhba pipeline running through Ukraine was used to ship oil to the Black Sea. Ukrtatnafta was responsible for running the Druzhba pipeline trunk and network in Ukraine, where a quarter of the natural gas consumed in Europe used to travel before arriving in the European Union. The conflict between Russia and Ukraine has diminished some of these numbers.

Because Ukraine has less natural resources than the Russian land mass, its oil and gas industries are not a mirror image of Russia's, although Ukraine oil and gas industries remain a mix of state and privately owned assets. As mentioned earlier, undiscovered Black Sea reserves may dramatically change this dynamic and will certainly require a different skill set within the Ukraine petroleum and gas sector.

For example, Naftohaz is a state-owned company under Ukraine's Ministry of Fuel and Energy. The company is involved with extraction, transportation, and refinement both natural gas and crude oil. Ukrtransgaz is today a Naftohaz subsidiary and still runs Ukraine's system of natural gas pipelines and underground gas depots. Another subsidiary of Naftohaz, Gas of Ukraine, is responsible for domestic gas distribution to local heating companies.

Naftohaz owns much of the pipeline and processing infra-

structure delineated above. The company is a major Ukrainian

employer with 175,000 workers, and has enjoyed $6 billion in

subsidies through Ukrainian domestic bonds from 2009 to 2012.

Former PricewaterhouseCoopers management consultant Andriy

Kobolyev took over as CEO of Naftohaz after the 2014 Euromaidan

revolution, hoping to reduce the country's dependence on Russian

gas while simultaneously reforming the company's business prac-

tices. (Wikipedia)

In turn, Naftohaz owns 43.1% of Ukrtatnafta, a smaller firm

with 4000 employees but substantial capacity as a Ukrainian pro-

ducer of oil products. Ukrtatnafta, run by Ukrainian oligarch,

CEO Serhiv Glushko, operates the Kremenchuk oil refinery (with a capacity of 368,500 BBL/day) as well as several petrol stations. Wikipedia reports Tatneft owns 8.6% of Ukrtatnafta while the government of Tatarstan owns 28.8% (in addition to the Naftohaz shares). Disputes about ownership had to be resolved in international court after 18% of the shares of Ukrtatnafta were transferred to two offshore companies.

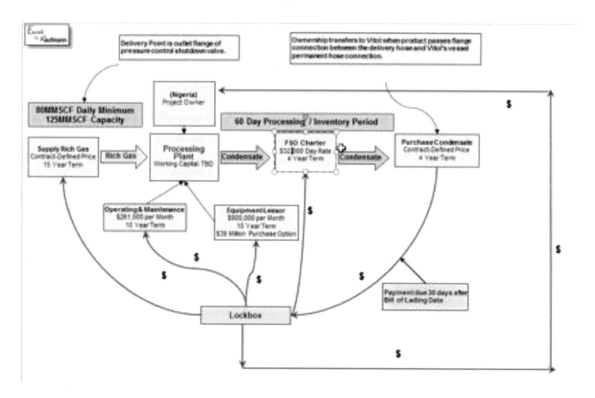

Running successful pipeline and refinery businesses requires the ability to acquire unrefined oil (high as possible quality) for low cost, innovative production processes and strong marketing and sales to maximize revenues from gasoline and various refinery products. Ukraine is not necessarily

locked to Russian supply for inputs, although oil transport

costs may be less if Russia supplies inputs.

Gas Stream
Units: USD 000

Gas and Refining Company
version 1.4

	Type of Gas Stream	Lean ▼	Reference
GS1	Daily Volume (MMSCF)	125	User Input
GS2	Total Moles in Gas Stream	329,446	Calculated *
GS3	HHV (Btu / Ft³)	1,252	User Input
GS4	LHV (Btu / Ft³)	1,135	User Input
GS5	Metric Tons Per Day	557	C - Calculations Column P
GS6	Total Metric Tons Per Year	203,378	GS5 x 365
GS7	Days to Reach 200,000 Metric Tons	359	200,000 ÷ GS5
GS8	Gallons per Day - Spec	267,169	C - Calculations Column R
GS9	Gallons per Day - Off-Spec	126,000	GS12 x 42
GS10	Gallons per Day - Total	393,169	GS8 + GS9
GS11	Barrels Per Day - Spec	6,361	GS8 ÷ 42
GS12	Barrels Per Day - Off-Spec	3,000	User Input
GS13	Barrels Per Day - Total	9,361	GS11 + GS12

*Total Moles Calculation: 14.696 x Daily Volume x 1,000,000
1 x 10.732 x (60 + 459.57)

Year	Revenues	Operating Profit	Net Profit	Annual NPV	Annual IRR
2005	102,177	53,141	39,711	33,571	-26%
2006	102,177	44,189	33,323	22,757	24%
2007	102,177	44,088	33,546	18,308	46%
2008	102,177	43,827	33,660	14,684	56%
2009	102,177	62,670	49,077	16,775	63%
2010	102,177	62,988	49,696	13,573	66%
2011	102,177	62,988	50,082	10,932	68%
2012	102,177	62,988	50,391	8,792	70%
2013	102,177	62,988	50,391	7,029	70%
2014	102,177	62,670	50,136	5,592	70%
2015	102,177	62,670	50,136	4,471	70%
Total	1,123,943	625,209	490,149	156,483	

Investment	Project NPV	Project IRR
57,000	156,483	70%

Ukraine's six oil refineries have a combined crude oil re
fining capacity estimated as of 1 January 2004 at 1.05 mil
lion barrels per day. However, domestic consumption of re
fined oil products is just over 30% of capacity, and <the
refineries> have even had problems securing enough crude
oil to supply the country's needs. (encyclopedia.com)

Thus, conflict will naturally arise between Ukraine oil/gas

processing interests and natural resource supply from Russia.

Ukraine interest in maximum flexibility to sell its oil refinery

products worldwide, including to the European Union, may also

run counter to Putin/Russian interest.

In the early 2000's, Ukraine proven oil reserves estimated at a mere 395 million barrels (Oil and Gas Journal). In 2003 and 2004, oil production was estimated at 86,800 barrels per day and 86,000 barrels per day, respectively, with consumption outstripping output for both years. In 2003, demand for oil averaged an estimated 415,000 barrels per day, and at an estimated 422,000 barrels per day in 2004. Net imports of oil in 2003 were estimated at 328,200 barrels per day, and at an estimated 336,000 barrels per day in 2004.

Imports in 2003 accounted for around 80% of demand, most of which came from Russia, with exploited reserves concentrated in the eastern Dnieper-Donetsk basin-- a fact that has not escaped the attention of Vladimir Putin, and certainly was a component of the Russian decision to seize that area. Black Sea deep water reserves can change this import/export ratio substantially.

Exploiting the deep water reserves will require drilling expertise that Ukraine does not have at this writing. Other geological science is key to a successful industry, and Ukraine's six refineries may require upgrade to maximize output and minimize polluting byproducts—or at least minimize the environmental and social impact of byproducts deemed poisonous or dangerous.

Geology, drilling and refinery expertise aren't the only requirements for successful exploitation of the deep water reserves. The complexity of petroleum industry outputs, products and markets requires a mastery of big data tools and data science. Modern business leaders frequently complain that obtaining data has become less of a problem: the analytical challenge has shifted to managing the overwhelming quantity of data available. Ukraine oil industry staff must parse market options for where product outputs might be most competitive, track trends in product pricing and monetize risk associated with anti-carbon protests and resulting market impact.

Data science specialists must extract and obtain data from multiple sources, transform the data into usable form (remove redundancies that warp analytic results and convert data to consistent formats so available tools can address it all), then present resulting analysis so product development, marketing and sales staff can bring the right products to ready markets. Given active government programs in most markets, Ukraine government officials must also be able to fashion trade agreements based on these evolving capabilities.

At the writing of this third edition, IEA has revised estimates of Ukraine oil reserves upward to 9 billion metric tons. At present, Ukraine consumes 10.6 metric tons, of which 10.4 tons are imported. Assuming that effective exploration and extraction can be performed, Ukraine's 6 or 7 refineries ought to be able to process 35 or 40 tons per year, leaving 25 or 30 tons per year for export or (conservatively) 175 million barrels of crude. Admittedly, quality of crude varies.

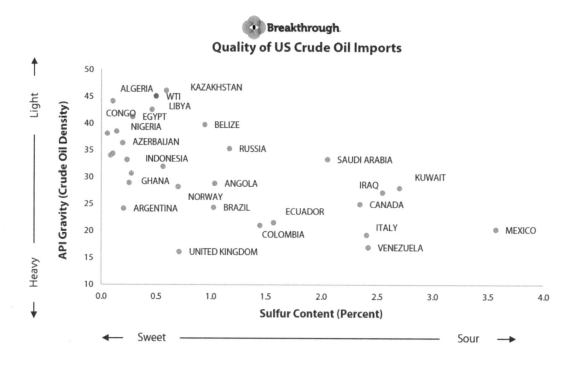

www.breakthroughfuel.com/blog/refined-products-outputs

Seventy percent of refined oil produces gasoline (roughly 20 gallons per barrel) and diesel fuel (10 gallons per barrel). At prices of $2/gallon and $3/gallon respectively, we might expect 175 million barrels of oil to augment Ukraine's economy an additional $12B per year. This GNP boost does not reflect that 2 gallons of hydrocarbon gas liquids (which produce rubber and plastic products, among others) per barrel and 6 gallons of "other products" can be sold for uses such as cosmetics.

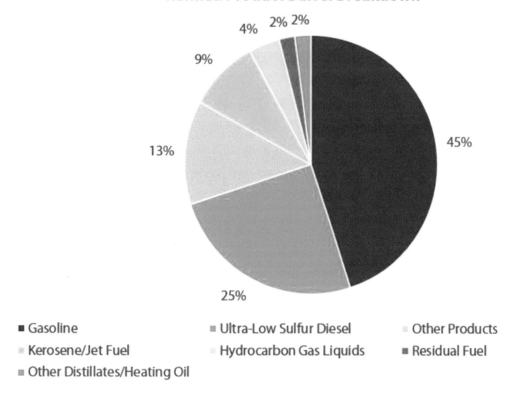

Refined Product Barrel Breakdown

45%

25%

13%

9%

4%

2% 2%

- ■ Gasoline
- ■ Ultra-Low Sulfur Diesel
- ■ Other Products
- ■ Kerosene/Jet Fuel
- ■ Hydrocarbon Gas Liquids
- ■ Residual Fuel
- ■ Other Distillates/Heating Oil

www.breakthroughfuel.com/blog/crude-oil-barrel/

The European cosmetics industry is a €79B ($95B US) juggernaut. Although the mark-up in cosmetics may range up to 50%, even a 5% slice of that constitutes a market of over $2B US for Ukraine's 1B gallons of "other product" from its projected petroleum refining industry.

Some of the common ingredients in beauty products that are petrochemical-derived include:

- Parafin wax
- Mineral oil
- Toluene
- Benzene
- Anything with *PEG* (polyethylene glycol)
- Anything with *DEA* (diethanolamine) or *MEA* (ethanolamine)
- Butanol and any word with *butyl*: butyl alcohol, butylparaben, butylene glycol
- EDTA (ethylenediaminetetraacetic acid)
- Any word with *propyl*—isopropyl alcohol, propylene glycol, propyl alcohol, cocamidopropyl betaine
- Parfum or fragrance—95 percent of chemicals used in fragrance are from petroleum. This one word can contain many, many chemicals that don't need to be listed and are likely endocrine disrupters.

https://goop.com/beauty/hair/goop-staffers-beauty-favorites/

##

According to its Ukraine article written in 2004, encyclopedia.com cited proven natural gas reserves at 39.6 trillion cu ft (citing <u>Oil and Gas Journal</u>). Consumption of natural gas has outpaced production in Ukraine, although development of Black Sea reserves may alter this dynamic as we expect it will change Ukraine from a net oil consumer to a net producer.

Natural gas disputes between Russia and Ukraine began in 2005, when Russia claimed Ukraine had been diverting natural gas intended for European use. These claims ultimately proved true, and disputes regarding funds due Russia escalated (including a complete shut-off of gas due to the European Union in 2008). The scandal continued to run into 2012, implicating both Ukraine president (and Petro Poroshenko mentor) Viktor Yushchenko and Orange political star and first woman elected prime minister in Ukraine, Iulia Tymoshenko.

##

Although some of the most onerous ethical lapses in United States business environment were not energy related, with the internet (2000) and real estate (2008) bubbles coming immediately to mind, corruption in the energy sector is not unknown in the US (ENRON being the best example). Under a capitalist model, businesses are often created to make a profit, rewarding owners, and, when publicly owned, shareholders-- the more profitable, the better.

We may praise our public servants in the United States, including the military, law enforcement, teachers and (in a pandemic world) health providers, but we worship our high earning sports, music and film stars, money-making gurus and beauty queens… both for their accomplishments in his/her chosen field, but often in unrelated personal and policy arenas. How is a child to make an ethical decision about a life path… and what sort of behavior do we accept from an adult seeking "rock star" status?

"Obey the law" seems an appropriate baseline, although we consistently watch people "at the top of the pyramid" taking advantage of loopholes in the law, being bailed out when economics (or a pandemic) goes sideways, while most of us are stuck paying our taxes or being held to a merciless standard when a pandemic, a new trend in process, economics or even geo-politics, make a mockery of our own careful planning and long-time hard work.

In his popular book <u>Reclaiming Virtue</u>, John Bradshaw suggests five pillars: 1) Do no harm; 2) Act in a fair fashion; 3) Be loyal to your group; 4) Respect (legitimate) authority; and 5) Be pure, clean and holy. Was Hunter Biden's decision to accept a lavishly paid role on the board of a small Ukraine natural gas company, Burisma, a violation of any of these pillars, or of any law? Are there implications for selecting Hunter's dad, Joe, to be our next President, that we ought to consider given this dynamic? Was Donald Trump wrong in asking Volodimyr Zelenskiy to investigate the legality of Hunter's role on Burisma's board?

There are certainly legal dimensions of these questions: were United States, Ukraine or international laws violated? From a moral perspective, what is fair? And when does loyalty go too far? Ultimately, I have not done new investigative research for this printing and must concede that facts in today's highly charged, politicized, environment are increasingly hard to validate.

Donald Trump has been and continues to be accused of "spinning his truth," but admittedly such spin is common practice in the political realm (and in business, where the Donald spent most of his career). "Spin" is not illegal, nor is political hyperbole (whether you choose to call that "inciting" or something else). The FDA, the Better Business Bureau and the SEC are charged with closing down businesses that don't meet a minimum standard, but the ranks of the world's wealthiest people (and the Fortune 100) are filled with those who exploited a gray (even not so gray) area. People appreciate integrity and reward people and companies they learn they can trust… but sometimes, admittedly, nice guys finish last.

Unfortunately, in a competitive world, the air waves (and the calendars of those in leadership) are filled with "spin" messaging, often to the detriment of more important topics. Sometimes spin messages are just more interesting than policy questions we might otherwise deem much more important… but some-times, it would seem, our leadership and others charged with policy formulation never get far enough down the priority list to fully consider important policy options, have the time to plan effective responses to key problems or, most importantly, orchestrate workable response implementations, whether legislation, executive order, task force or business initiative.

##

Ukraine fuel resources and infrastructure are not limited to oil and gas. Ukraine has substantial coal reserves, although not enough to satisfy its industrial requirements for the resource. Hydroelectric dams produce slightly less than half of the nuclear power Ukraine produces: in spite of being home to the worst nuclear disaster in world history (Chernobyl), Ukraine was producing 40% of the its electricity requirements that way (at least according to research at this writing).

##

Some would say the petrol economy is a relic, that will soon be replaced with alternative forms of energy. While the advent of electric automobiles for consumers has been dramatic in recent years, power generation in general has continued to be primarily carbon-based across the world and certainly in Ukraine.

Greta Thunberg calls for an end to carbon production and consumption.

Although advanced economies are observing global warming statistics and reviewing options for reducing the carbon economy, a substantial percentage of the production of carbon results from international air and sea traffic. Trucking also produces a significant percentage of the content. While automobiles with electric engines are on the market, electric trucks have just hit the market (at this writing, trucking fleets do not reflect this initiative at all, much less in a meaningful way). Electric engines powering aircraft and ships for freight are not yet available. Since carbon content saturates many modern industries (including the power industries that charge those electric engine batteries), elimination of the internal combustion engine may not actually provide a "net, net" reduction in carbon related pollutants.

Although he conceded that calculating pollution emissions from air travel is immensely complicated due to type aircraft, length and altitude of flight among other factors, an article the Clark Williams-Derry wrote in 2007, inspired the following comment:

There is no IPCC emissions scenario that is sustainable that can be met if people keep flying at all. Monbiot in Heat does the math as do many other groups and scientists. So until anyone anywhere comes up with way for high-speed air travel to continue for even a couple more decades, the only question is how soon we will kick our habit and leave some emissions room for things like agriculture, power, shipping, industry and so on. Also flying has lots of multiplying factors that make it much worse. There are the IPCC documented ones (i've read the report and lots more in detail):* NOx & Ozone which equals CO2 in warming* Carbon soot* Vapour trails* Cloud formation* Water vapor… (Barry's Comment to Williams-Derry article)

Add to this pollution delivered from shipping:

…ships get bigger, the pollution is getting worse. The most staggering statistic of all is that just 16 of the world's largest ships can produce as much lung-clogging sulphur pollution as all the world's cars… their colossal engines, each as heavy as a small ship… use as much fuel as small power stations…. unlike power stations or cars, they can burn the cheapest, filthiest, high-sulphur fuel: the thick residues left behind in refineries after the lighter liquids have been taken. The stuff nobody on land is allowed to use. (http://www.dailymail.co.uk/science-tech/article-1229857/How-16-ships-create-pollution-cars-world.html#ixzz4J0zcUZcZ)

Organizations like Climate Action Network Europe (www.caneurope.org) track this type of data on an on-going basis.

In any event, the global carbon economy will persist for the indefinite future, and global economies (like that in

Ukraine) will depend on oil and natural gas inputs for at least another generation.

Chocolate

Jared Diamond's book, <u>Guns</u>, <u>Germs</u> <u>and</u> <u>Steel</u>, highlights the importance of native grains in the development of nations, attributing a half dozen crops to Europe and none to the Americas and Africa. Diamond points out that wheat enabled specialization within human societies, enabling development of sophisticated government and standing armies. Today, corn, wheat and barley make up over $20B of Ukraine's $580B economy. Chocolate adds up to over $1B of Ukraine's GNP.

Although oil and gas are significant economic drivers, the Ukraine economy has a broader base than most. It's heavy manufacturing supplied the Soviet Armed Forces and space program, while outsourcing software houses have customers across the globe (including within the United States). Even chocolate flows contribute substantially to the economy, and to the personal leadership viability of Ukraine's president at the time this book was first published, Petro Poroshenko.

Ukraine's Maidan revolution ushered Petro Poroshenko into office. Speaking for Ukrainians at large, Kateryna Kruk writes: "We wanted a free society built on universal values. We wanted a just state based on rule of law. We held our ground in the square at the heart of Kiev not because we wanted another rotation of political elites but because we needed to see systemic changes in the way our country was run." She also concedes, "The ideals of Maidan were so comprehensive and ambitious that we should use them as a roadmap for change in Ukraine in a much longer narrative."

In 2013, crowds around Ukraine began taking to the streets, calling for closer ties to the European Union and measures to fight corruption within Ukraine. Russian ties to Ukraine's government at the time, led by President Viktor Yanukovych, reinforced the government with loans and armed henchmen to put down the protests. In response to this, Ukraine's parliament, the historic Verkhovna Rada, voted to impeach Yanukovych, and installed its speaker, Oleksandr Turchenov, as interim president until elections could be held in May. Petro Poroshenko emerged victorious when the elections were held.

Petro Poroshenko isn't your ordinary chocolate magnate. His father was a plant manager and young Petro (like Vladimir Putin) received some early renown as a practitioner of Sambo and Judo. Poroshenko received a degree in economics from Kiev State University, where he met and befriended the future president of Georgia, Mikhail Saakasvili. Poroshenko continued his involvement with the university for some years, having also started a legal advisory firm that supplied cocoa beans to the Soviet chocolate industry.

In 1993, Poroshenko teamed with his father and several other businessmen to found UkrPromInvest Ukrainian Industry and Investment Company, then successfully ran for parliament in 1998. In the years leading to Poroshenko's parliamentary run, UkrPromInvest acquired control over several state-owned confectionery enterprises, including factories in Bershad, Kiev, Vinnytsia, Mariupol and Kremenchuk as well as foreign factories in Klaipeda, Lithuania and Lipetsk, Russia. The single company that emerged is called "Roshen." UkrPromInvest has interests in various types of firms (not only confectionery), while Poroshenko also receives some notoriety for his ownership of the 5 Kanal television channel.

Poroshenko first gained election as a member of Social Democratic Party of Ukraine (the party of the second president of the country), but broke off to form his own "Solidarity" party, ultimately heading Viktor Yuschenko's campaign for president. Viktor won the presidency of Ukraine in 2005. Poroshenko was appointed to various posts in Yuschenko's government, but was also tainted in various scandals in those years. He was reelected to Parliament in 2006, but wasn't successful in leadership bids there and opted not to run for another term in 2007.

According to Forbes, Poroshenko attained billionaire status in the early 2000's but has suffered some financial set-backs in recent years due to general Ukraine economic malaise and specific Russian actions against Roshen, Poroshenko's chocolate company.

Yuschenko rehabilitated Poroshenko in 2009, appointing him Foreign Minister and then to the National Security and Defense Council, where Poroshenko pushed for Ukraine membership of NATO. In 2012 Poroshenko again ran for Parliament, this time as an independent candidate (district number 12), winning election with 70% of the vote.

Poroshenko actively supported the Euromaidan protests between November 2013 and February 2014, and stated in an interview, "From the beginning, I was one of the organizers of the Maidan. My television channel — Channel 5 — played a tremendously important role.... At that time, Channel 5 started to broadcast, there were just 2,000 people on the Maidan. But during the night, people went by foot — seven, eight, nine, 10 kilometers — understanding this is a fight for Ukrainian freedom and democracy. In four hours, almost 30,000 people were there." ("Interview with Ukrainian Presidential Candidate," Washington Post, 4/25/2014).

Given this involvement, Poroshenko's success as a candidate for the presidency was not surprising. Although he initiated various reforms as president (including significant changes to police organizations in Kiev, for example), when the time came for re-election in 2019, a long list of candidates emerged to oppose Poroshenko, including a comedian whose television show made entertainment of corruption in Ukraine.

Iulia Timoshenko and Petro Poroshenko jockeyed for second place in the run-off for the presidency, but the comedian, Volodimyr Zelenskiy, won a crushing victory—again, on a platform of anti-corruption.

##

Archeologists and historians suggest that trading along the Dnipr would have begun with materials for tools: obsidian and flint… then copper, and bronze. Very early in prehistory, Ukraine was home to "… prosperous food gatherers… the mammoth hunters of the Ukraine." Singer, et al, editors. <u>A History of Technology: Volume I</u>. Oxford University Press: London, 1956. (p. 42)

Between the 5th and 3rd Centuries BC, spanning the 4th Century, when Diamond suggested Ukrainians domesticated the horse (<u>Guns</u>, <u>Germs</u> <u>and</u> <u>Steel</u>, p. 77), Ukraine inhabitants continued to trade prosperously, according to the Royal Ontario Museum in Canada (from its exhibit of Scythian gold in 2000):

The Scythians were a nomadic people who migrated from Kazakstan and prospered through trade along the north coast of the

Black Sea … [and] with the contemporary Greek civilizations..”
(http://info.goldavenue.com/info site/in who/in exhibi-
tions/in who nomads.html). It isn't completely clear whether
the Scythians produced these gold items, or provided Greek
craftsmen something in exchange for these items.

Like the Greeks, Mamluk craftsmen (with headquarters in
Cairo) needed substantial amounts of raw materials… and we imagine, food, both of which were available in abundance from
Ukraine. Historians record trade routes expanding from Greece
the Italian city states also: "Venice played a crucial role in
the trade of Islamic metalwork in the Mediterranean. Shipping
documents reveal that Venetians exported large quantities of
copper and brass to the Near East; in return, they imported fin-
ished inlaid vessels. Mamluk basins, ewers, candlesticks, and
incense burners found a place in the finest Venetian homes and
churches, and some were even customized with the coat of arms of
Venetian noble families. Local craftsmen admired the skill and
design of Islamic metalwork too and frequently imitated it."
https://www.metmuseum.org/toah/hd/vmos/hd vmos.htm

Metallurgy came to drive some of the decisions of Roman Emperor Tiberius (14-37 AD) with copper production happening up
until 400BC, brass and iron taking its place thereafter. "From
800 BC onwards iron came into use in central Europe on an increasing scale for weapons and tools." (Singer, et al, editors.

A History of Technology: Volume II, Oxford University Press: London, 1957, p55)

While history does not record much of the economic transactions suggested above, there are records of Ukraine leadership in the late 1600's. Ivan Mazeppa studied at Kyivan Mohyla College, then went to Warsaw to study at a Jesuit college there. He attracted the interest of the Polish king when serving at a page at the court of Jan II Casimir Vasa, and was sent by the king to study in Holland, learning gunnery there and traveling on to Germany, Italy, France and the Low Countries (Holland, then the premier commercial center in the world). http://www.encyclopediaofukraine.com/display.asp?linkpath=pages%5CM%5CA%5CMazepaIvan.htm

A visitor to Ukraine is struck by the number of buildings constructed by Ivan Mazeppa. We find no record of Ivan Mazeppa involvement in trade, and certainly Ivan Mazeppa's vast wealth wasn't the result of the arrival of the chocolate industry, since Dutch inventor and merchant Van Houten did not invent the chocolate press until a hundred years after Mazeppa's activities. (Carol Off. Bitter Chocolate. New York: The New Press, 2006. p. 47) The vast building program is hard to attribute to Mazeppa's service to various other governments alone, however. Perhaps serf labor, a farming system and associated capability to ship food stuffs to Europe, Africa and Russia would have generated the wealth required.

"During the nineteenth century, parallel to the Ottoman Empire' decline, the Black Sea region developed exceptionally, mainly due to the grain export and transports. The grain trade contributed to the fast growth of the port-cities on the Black Sea ring road which "created the urban zone of the northern and eastern coasts of the Black Sea" Harlaftis (1996). The Greeks, Jews, Armenians, Albanian and Bulgarians formed the main merchant community of the region and they could be found in every port-city of the Black Sea coast (Jensen and Rosegger, 1968; also Lyratzopouoou and Zarotiadis. "Black Sea: Old trade routes…" Procedia Economics and Finance 9, 2014, pp. 74-82).

In addition to serving as a key Naval base, Sevastopol, "the city of Russian Glory" (Plokhy, 2000), was established in 1783 in order to serve as a trading port and a naval base and bastion of the south Russian empire. Catherine the Great created the new city on the site of the ruins of the ancient Greek city Chersonesus, on the Black Sea coast of Crimea. Ultimately, merchant populations in the city were decimated during War War II, and the port primarily serves as a naval base today. (IBID)

During the nineteenth century, the city of Odessa constituted the most important port of the Black Sea region, with the cereals being the main trading export product between Black Sea region and Europe (predominantly Italy). (IBID) Although wars served to disrupt commerce, various merchants and salespeople from around the Mediterranean and Eastern Europe substantially helped increase trade from Odessa. (IBID)

During 1815-1824 approximately 709,371 chetverts of wheat were annually exported from the ports of Odessa, when the total wheat exports of Russia did not exceed 2,115,000 chetverts. Since 1866 and until 1868 wheat exports amounted 57% of Russia's total grain exports. 78% shipped from the Black Sea and Azov Sea, with more than 50% specifically shipping from Odessa. From 1806 to 1815 shipments departing from Odessa averaged 30,000 tons annually (mainly grain), while shipping jumped to 125,000 tons annually from 1815 to 1826. (IBID)

Ukraine has historically been one of the world's leading producers of iron ore, as well as a major world producer of fer-roalloys, ilmenite, steel, and manganese ore (with 75% of the former Soviet Union's reserves). The mining and metallurgical industry employed 500,000 persons; 270,000 worked in ironmaking, steelmaking, and ferroalloys enterprises. In 2002, over 60% by value of Ukraine's $18 billion in exports came from the "mineral products" category. Ferrous and nonferrous metals were Ukraine's top export commodities in 2002. Fuel and petroleum products were the country's second-leading commodities export (encyclopedia.com).

Ukraine's steppe region in the south was once one of the most fertile regions in the world. Ukraine's famous humus-rich black soil accounts for one-third of the world's black soil and holds great potential for agricultural production. However, the soil is rapidly losing its fertility due to improper land and crop management. Ukraine typically produced over half of the sugar beets and one-fifth of all grains grown for the former USSR. In addition, two of the largest vegetable-oil research centers in the world are at Odessa and Zaporizhzhya. This agroindustry accounts for one-third of agricultural employment. To some extent, however, agroindustrial development has been hampered by the deteriorating environment as well as a shortage of investment funds due to the aftermath of the nuclear power plant disaster at Chernobyl. (encyclopedia.com)

Early Soviet policy allowed for cultural autonomy and local administration by Ukrainian Communists. But Stalin changed this liberal policy in the 1930s when he initiated strict Russification and persecution of Ukrainian nationalists. This policy culminated in the Soviet-engineered famine of 1932–33 that resulted in the death of 7 to 10 million Ukrainians. (encyclopedia.com)

There is a wide railroad network in Ukraine (according to encyclopedia.com, 22,473 km (13,988 mi) in 2002). Highways in 2002 totaled 169,679 km (105,540 mi), of which 164,249 km (102,162 mi) are hard-surfaced, including 1,770 km (1,100 mi) of expressways. In 2003, there were 5,603,800 passengers cars and 985,700 commercial vehicles registered for use. (encyclope-dia.com)

The main marine ports are Berdyansk, Illichivsk, Kerch, Kherson, Mariupol, Mykolayiv, Odessa, and Sevastopol. The merchant marine fleet had 201 ships of 1,000 GRT or over, for a total capacity of 675,904 GRT in 2005. (encyclopedia.com)

Then, "in the mid-1950's, … Malcom McLean hit on the idea of packing cargoes into enormous steel boxes— shipping containers." (Winchester, Atlantic, p. 350). Before then, loading "a ton of cargo by hand cost nearly six dollars, while to do so on a containerized ship… cost only sixteen cents." (IBID p. 351). In spite of this shipping innovation, during the 20th Century the oil trade increased remarkably (as delineated in the previous chapter) and Odessa was transformed into more of an oil port while grain exports continued declining. (IBID)

Water transport continued to improve under the Communists, complementing historic and modern land transport systems. Ukraine has 1,672 km (1,040 mi) of navigable inland waterways as of 2004. The Dnipro River is the primary inland waterway, but the Danube, western Pivd Buh, Pryp'yat', and Desna are also used for import-export traffic. (encyclopedia.com) "The construction of the river Danube – Black Sea Canal, that began in 1978 and concluded in 1984, contributed significantly to the growth of the region …. The main product dispatched is oil and its products (Turnock, 1986).

In the late twentieth century, eight of the Black Sea countries experienced a transition period that led to the region's general decline, at least in the short- and medium-run. The last decade of the century brought stability in the region, political and economic security and in some cases also economic growth. Between the years 2000 and 2008 the region was characterized by "high and sustained growth", with increasing living standards, and high levels of trade and investment. Unfortunately, the worldwide financial meltdown that occurred in late 2008 drove the collapse of many financial markets, with associated impact on the growth of the Black Sea region. (IBID)

L & Z argue that restarting the growth enjoyed among the Black Sea ports and surrounding areas requires creative collaboration among the many countries involved. Guavas (2010) specifically highlights areas which enable comparative advantage of one area over another. Those areas include energy, transport, finance, telecommunications and environment. Gains among the region's economies are essential in order for trade to grow inside the Black Sea region. Various policies facilitate trade, including elimination of dual taxation, and agreements for investments which drive gains between the economies. (IBID)

Construction of the Black Sea Canal, and many of the other initiatives advocated by L&Z support a robust economy—one that enables innovation because one sector or another cannot dominate. A global technical community has devised a system for removing the hegemony of the banking community and for transferring resources without such a dependency. The system, called "blockchain," provides a digital record of transactions, with individual, possibly encrypted, and also uneditable ("immutable") records (called "blocks") that are linked together in a single list ("chain").

Chocolate provides a useful illustration of the benefits of blockchain technology. The primary ingredient of chocolate, cocoa beans, are predominantly sourced from a few nations on the African continent.

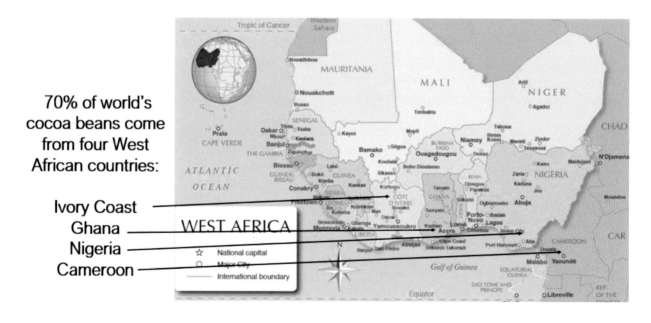

These countries are poor and the people involved in growing and harvesting cocoa beans receive a very small percentage of the ultimate revenue of a chocolate product.

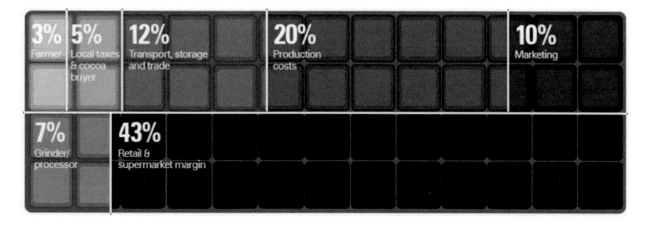

Blockchain technology might insure better revenues for farmer/producers, much as it has in certain coffee distributors, where a coffee drinking customer may "tip" the grower from his/her hand held phone. Cryptocurrencies (such as bitcoin) are a key component of the blockchain solution, but the international community is still grappling with how to adopt cryptocurrencies and otherwise capitalize on the promises of blockchain.

One company that has already delivered implementations to support food (and food ingredients/markets) is www.chainpoint.org.

##

In 1991, with the Soviet economy in free fall due to a drop in oil prices to $10/bbl and many Socialist Republics in various stages of secession from the Soviet Union, a "gang of eight" attempted a coup against Gorbachev in Moscow. Ukraine president Leonid Kravchuck and Belarusian parliament chair Stanislav Shushkevich met with Boris Yeltsin, who had been elevated to president of the Russian SSR. They declared the Soviet Union dissolved and established the Commonwealth of Independent States through what became known as the Belavezha Accords.

Yeltsin returned to Moscow and blocked the coup, soon taking control of the government in the Kremlin, in the name of the Russian state. Sobchak, Putin's employer at the time and mayor of "Peter" (then still called Leningrad), supported Yeltsin. Kravchuk would remain President of Ukraine for two terms, defeated in his third reelection bid by Leonid Kuchma in 1994 (who went on to win a second five year term as president in 1999).

Kuchma had graduated from the Dnipropetrovsk National University with a degree in aerospace engineering. When he was 38, Kuchma became Communist party head at the Yuzhny machine building plant, serving on the Central Committee of the Ukraine Communist Party and as a delegate to several congresses of the Communist Party of the Soviet Union. Kuchma began criticizing the Communist Party in the late 1980's, ultimately joining the Verkhovna Rada in 1990, and became Prime Minister in 1992.

Although he called for closer ties to the European Union from time to time, Kuchma won his first presidential term promising to rebuild the economy through improved trade with Russia and faster market reforms within Ukraine. His presidency was accused of strong arm tactics, including the killing of a journalist in 2000.

After a career in banking, including Vice Chair of the JSC Agroindustrial Bank Ukraine and Chairman of the National Bank of Ukraine (Ukraine's Central Bank), Viktor Yushchenko was appointed Prime Minister by Kuchma in 1999. He used this platform to wage a successful bid for the presidency in 2004, including Iulia Tymoshenko in his government, although voting scandals plagued that election.

Yuschenko capitalized on a popular "Orange Revolution" movement to win office, but immediately following election his popularity plummeted due to continued charges of corruption within the government, including Orange Revolution notables, like Iulia Tymoshenko. Attempting rapprochement with Russia, Yuschenko appointed his opponent, Victor Yanukovych, as new prime minister. Parliamentary crises dominated the Yuschenko presidency and resulted in a modification to the Ukraine constitution limiting the ability of the president to dismiss parliament.

Yanukovych built close ties to Russia as prime minister from 2002 to 2004 and again from 2006 to 2007. He won election to the presidency against Iulia Tymoshenko in 2010, but his work to obtain subsidies and tighten economic ties with Russia ran counter to popular interest in the European Union trade agreement, resulting in Yanukovych ouster via the Maidan Revolution, in 2014.

##

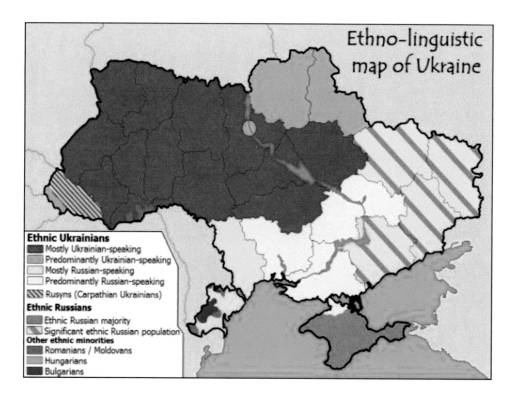

On May 2014, in response to a referendum within Crimea which resulted in Russian annexation of the territory, President Obama announced sanctions on individuals in Putin's staff and others supporting the Russian government. Obama called the referendum and annexation a clear violation of the Ukraine constitution and international law.

Some months before this, The Associated Press reported 80 unmarked military vehicles on the move in rebel-controlled areas in Ukraine's Donbass region. An OSCE Special Monitoring Mission observed convoys of heavy weapons and tanks in DPR-controlled territory without insignia. Although senior leadership of the United States Army attribute the Crimean and Donbass actions as brilliant Russian proxy battles (resulting in very little resource expenditure), a former Pentagon strategy adviser suggested in early November 2014 that there were as many as 7,000 Russian troops inside Ukraine, while OSCE monitors stated they observed vehicles transporting ammunition and soldiers' dead bodies crossing the Russian-Ukrainian border under the guise of humanitarian aid convoys.

The Crimean annexation had been a Russian response to the European Trade pact that had finally been presented through the European Union after Yulia Tymoshenko and Yuriy Lutsenko were released from prison. EU announcements labeled these imprison-

ments (among other actions) "a stark deterioration of democracy

and rule of law." In response, Ukraine released the prisoners

and enacted various other electoral, judicial and constitutional

reforms.

For some two years, elements in Ukraine worked to emplace a

Trade Association agreement with the European Union. Then on

November 26th, 2013, Vladimir Putin announced that such an

agreement would be "bad for Russian security interests." In the

months leading to its formulation within the European Union or-

ganization, Russia had proposed an alternate including a Russia-

Ukraine-European Union clearing house or a customs union between

Belarus, Kazakhstan, and Russia.

In response, the Yankovich government suspended prepara-

tions for signing of association agreement, instead proposing the creation of a three-way trade commission between Ukraine, the European Union and Russia that would resolve trade issues between the sides. President Vyctor Yankovich reluctance to sign the Ukraine-EU agreement resulted in protests, European posturing and, ultimately, his ouster and the election (on 25 May 2014) of a new president, Petro Poroshenko.

##

Pundits suggest that ethnolinguistic dynamics in Ukraine will no longer divide the country, and that Russian aggression is widely condemned within Ukraine. In addition, Ukraine has managed a strong defense against the Russian "bear," although perhaps not strong enough should Putin choose a full invasion of the rest of the country.

> Ukraine was able to quickly organize an impressive national army, in part because it had always been an important contributor to the Soviet armed forces. In 2005 Ukranian armed forces numbered 187,600 active personnel with 1,000,000 reservists. Ground forces (Army) numbered 125,000 (continued) and was organized into three commands and a number of specialized brigades and regiments of artillery, special forces, air defense, rocket and missile, and attack helicopter units. It was equipped with 3,784 main battle tanks, 600 reconnaissance vehicles, 3,043 armored infantry fighting vehicles, 8,492 armored personnel carriers, and 3,705 artillery pieces. The Air Force and Air Defense Force had a combined total of 49,100 active personnel, that operated 444 combat capable aircraft, including 26 bombers, 280 fighters, and 187 fighter ground attack aircraft. The Air Defense force was outfitted with 825 surface-to-air missile batteries. (encyclopedia.com)

The oligarchs in Ukraine haven't only been busy building fortunes: they have also been hiring soldiers.

Paramilitary forces included an estimated 39,900 internal security troops, 45,000 border guards, 14,000 coast guard personnel, and more than 9,500 civil defense troops. The Ukraine participated in missions in eight foreign countries or regions. The defense budget for 2005 was $1.09 billion.
(encyclopedia.com)

ГДЕ ДИСЛОЦИРОВАНЫ ВООРУЖЕННЫЕ СИЛЫ УКРАИНЫ

Ukraine was assured that its territorial integrity would be preserved by all five permanent members of the United Nations Security Council (Russia, United States, United Kingdom, China and France) when it transferred all its nuclear weapons to Russia after the Soviet Union dissolved. Unfortunately those assurances haven't stopped Russian adventurism and haven't inspired any of these nations, including the United States, to take substantive action to counter-act the Russian moves. (Andreas Umland. "The Ukraine Example: Nuclear Disarmament doesn't pay." World Affairs. Winter 2016.)

##

Volodymyr Zelenskiy was born in Kryvyi Rih, Ukraine, on January 25th, 1978. His grandfather served in the 57th Guards Motorized Rifle Division (MRD), of the Soviet Union's Red Army. His great-grandfather and three of Zelenskiy's grandfather's brothers were killed in the Holocaust. Zelenskiy's father heads the department of cybernetics and computing hardware at Kryyvi Rih Institute of Economics. His mother worked as an engineer.

Volodymyr Zelenskiy earned a law degree from Kryvyi Rih Institute of Economics, but has never practiced law. He participated in a comedy competition at 17 years old, leading to the formation of a comedy troop, Kvartahl 95, which later became a company that produced TV shows for Ukrainian channel One + One, and was ultimately absorbed by TV channel "Inter." His most visible qualification for serving as president of Ukraine was (all comedy aside) that he played one on television.

Zelenskiy's character receives briefing on renaming Ukraine regional districts ("Servant of the People" show).

Shortly after the start of the conflict in Donbass, Kvartal 95 donated one million hryvnias to the Ukrainian army, resulting in a groundswell against Zelenskiy in Russia. Zelenskiy has continued to produce shows and star in both movies and TV shows up until the beginning of his political career, which Wikipedia notes began with the founding of the "Servant of the People"

party in March 2018. Zelenskiy declared his candidacy for president on New Year's Eve, 2018.

Zelenskiy ran a very effective social media campaign leading up to the run-off election, where he attracted over 30 percent of the vote. Petro Poroshenko, the incumbent, took second
place with 16 percent, while Iulia Timoshenko, the country's
first woman prime minister, came in third at 13 percent.

Claims have surfaced regarding Zelenskiy ties to billionaire Ihor Kolomoysky, leading partner of the Privat Group and
former governor of the Dnipropetrovsk oblast, however Zelenskiy
continued to criticize Poroshenko for his ties to an inner cir-
cle of oligarchs thru the general election.

Since winning the general election for president with 73
percent of the vote on April 21st, 2019, and his inauguration on
May 20th, Zelenskiy has enjoyed congratulations and support
across Europe and the United States. He appointed many col-
leagues from Kvartahl 95 to his administration and invited former president of Ukraine Leonid Kuchma to join a Tripartite Con-
tact Group seeking settlement to the Donbass conflict.

Zelenskiy dismissed governors of 15 of Ukraine's oblasts
along with 5 oblast secret service heads in June 2019, then won
a resounding victory in the July 21st parliamentary election
(via the "Servant of the People" party). Thus, a new Honcharuk
government emerged at the end of August 2019, to aid Zelenskiy

efforts to improve the Ukraine economy and de-escalate tension

with Russia. A "Shmyhal" government replaced Honcharuk in March

2020.

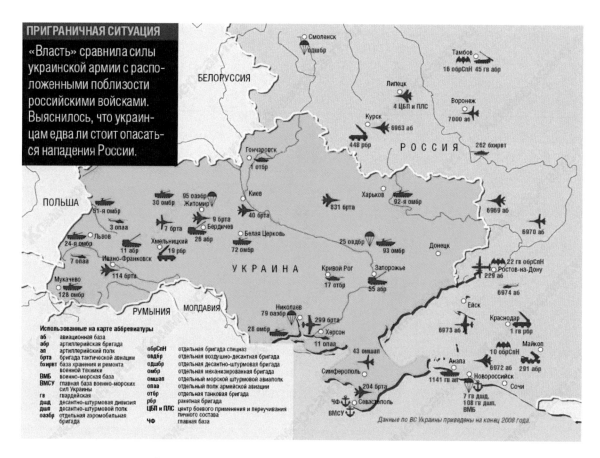

Forces estimates and placement on Ukraine's border

Zelenskiy remains committed to financial and domestic re-

forms, took a phone call from then-President Donald Trump re-

garding allegations surrounding Hunter Biden's involvement with

the Burisma company and has suggested presenting membership of

NATO and the European Union to Ukraine via referendum. Zelen-

skiy states that Ukraine is an independent nation, not a younger sister of Russia, although the Russia issue remains perhaps the most important tension in the country at this writing.

Russian Policy

On November 25th, 2018, a Ukrainian flotilla consisting of two gunboats and a tugboat sailed into the Kerch Strait headed for the Azov Sea and Ukrainian port, Mariupol. Ukraine claims Russia was notified in advance and refused to respond to radio coordination on the day of the incident. Russia claims the three vessels were behaving recklessly, did not request prior permission to enter what Russia claims as territorial waters after seizing Crimea, and that the Ukraine vessels refused to answer radio calls that day.

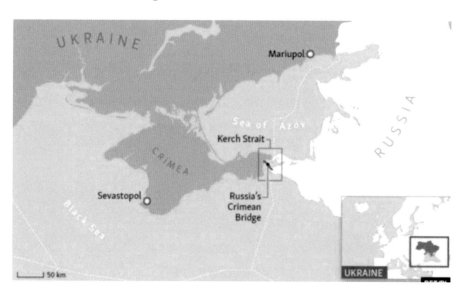

"Explainer: What the Kerch Strait skirmish tells us…," rferl.org, November 26, 2018.

In response to the flotilla, Russia scrambled various Federal Security Service coast guard vessels, two Sukhoi 30 fighter jets and two helicopters. Russia also placed a large cargo ship under the Crimean bridge, blocking the strait to subsequent traffic.

Ukraine president was still Petro Poroshenko, who decried the Russian response as an illegal response to vessels in international waters (since Ukraine doesn't recognize Crimea as legal, these waters are not acknowledged Russian waters). After the Russian response damaged the Ukraine vessels and injured a half-dozen Ukraine sailors, Poroshenko declared martial law (supporting his campaign slogan, "Army! Language! Faith!").

Russia ultimately seized the vessels and detained all twenty-four Ukraine crew. US Ambassador to the United Nations, Nikki Haley, condemned the Russian action as an "outrageous violation of Ukraine territory," while international condemnation included demands for release of the Ukraine vessels and sailors from the International Tribunal for Law of Sea in May 2019, and consideration of sanctions against Russia at the 2018 G20 Buenos Aires Summit (where US President Donald Trump canceled a previously scheduled meeting with Vladimir Putin because of the incident). The United States sent the USS Fort McHenry to patrol the Black Sea on January 10, 2019, then dispatched the USS Donald Cook on a similar mission on January 19, 2019.

Leading up to the incident, Russian propaganda claimed Ukraine was dredging the Azov Sea to prepare for NATO vessels, were planning to infect the Black Sea region with Cholera and were planning to blow up the Crimean bridge with a nuclear bomb. Ultimately, Russia allowed the Ukraine sailors to return home on September 7, 2019 and returned the captured vessels to Ukraine on November 18, 2019.

Although Putin claimed the incident was staged by Petro Poroshenko to bolster support for the upcoming election, as we detailed in the last chapter, Poroshenko was able to capture second place in the presidential run-off election, but lost the general election rather badly to comedian Volodimir Zelenskiy.

##

There are few adults in Russia today who are not familiar with the international nature of Communism. Although that ideology was certainly discredited upon dissolution of the Soviet Union in the early 1990's, Communist parties gave the Russian government credible inroads across South/Central America (and Cuba), while the united Arab Socialist, or Baath, Party provided ties (in Iraq before Sadaam Hussein's overthrow and still in Syria) in the Middle East.

Both Lenin and Stalin were convinced that a proletariat revolution would sweep Europe within days (certainly no longer than months) of the Russian Revolution. The Russian government had established ties with England under Peter the Great, then with France, in order to counter Germany and even a British-Japanese alliance. Russia became a major force in Europe through Peter the Great's victory over Sweden in the great Northern War, but its influence ebbed in the following centuries.

For decades, historians and Russian scholars recognize a certain insecurity apparently inherent to the Russian psyche. Of course, one might observe a number of substantial disasters that occurred in history, to support such a psyche: the defeat of the Russian Navy to the Japanese, the inability to build world class ships for its navy leading up to World War II, and the general melt down of the Russian economy that led to the collapse of the Soviet Union in early 1990.

Boris Yeltsin had been educated as an engineer and (after a number of years working in industry) ran the construction department in Sverdlovsk before being appointed first secretary of the Communist Party there. He was elected a member of the Central Committee of the Soviet Communist Party in 1981.

Because of the importance of Sverdlovsk Oblast to Soviet industry, Gorbachev brought Yeltsin to Moscow to head the Construction Department for the Soviet Union, joining a young(er)

117

team attempting to reinvigorate the Soviet economy. From there, Gorbachev appointed Yeltsin First Secretary of the CPSU Moscow City, also bringing him into the Politburo as a non-voting member. Yeltsin became popular with city residents for firing corrupt officials in the Moscow city bureaucracy. Unfortunately, he had a falling out with Gorbachev after complaining that reform efforts were moving too slowly.

Gorbachev ultimately removed Yeltsin from the Politburo and fired him as Mayor of Moscow. Miraculously, Yeltsin promptly ran for Congress of People's Deputies representing Moscow, winning with 92% of the vote. The next year Boris was elected to the Congress of People's Deputies of Russia (representing Sverdlovsk) with 72% of the vote. He was then elected President of the Presidium of the Russian SFSR (over Gorbachev objections), leaving Yeltsin in charge when the Soviet Union dissolved shortly thereafter.

Gorbachev had started a process for privatizing state assets that Yeltsin inherited. The privatization process was not only a critical ingredient for achieving an economy competitive in world markets, it became a significant source of influence within Russia as history evolved. Thus, Yeltsin's 1996 decision to bring Vladimir Putin to Moscow, in a role as deputy on the Presidential Property Management Department, proved fortuitous for Putin's career.

Vladimir Vladimirovich Putin was born on October 7, 1952, in St Petersburg. His father had served on submarines, then in the Red Army, in World War II. His grandfather was a cook for Stalin. Putin was a bit of a ruffian, and not a very good student ("a bad boy" in Putin's own words "autobio"), but channeled his energies into judo until resolving to enter the KGB in his early teens, scoring a law degree and Moscow judo championship en route to that goal.

When the Soviet Union dissolved in 1991, Vladimir Putin had been an adviser to the mayor of St Petersburg, Anatoly Sobchak, for a year. Although he was nominally still on the KGB payroll, Putin claims he knew his career in the KGB had become a dead end. When Sobchak lost reelection, Putin came to Yeltsin's attention and moved to Moscow. His privatization duties impressed Boris Yeltsin, who appointed the former KGB officer as his presidential deputy.

Thus, when Yeltsin stepped down, Vladimir Putin inherited a Russia riddled with insecurities. He also inherited one of the most resource rich nations in the world and, at least according to Wikipedia, one of the most innovative in the world, including the world's 15th highest patent application rate, the 8th highest concentration of high-tech (internet and aerospace, for example) public companies and the third highest graduation rate of scientists and engineers in the world.

Although Russian tactical formations may be imposing to Ukraine, overall NATO tactical capabilities exceed that of Russia, justifying maintenance and even modernizing the country's nuclear arsenal. Experts claim "US Military has no defense against Russian nuclear missiles…" as recently as April 2017 (Newsweek 4/5/2017). Russia signed the Biologic and Toxin Weapons Convention in 1972 but immediately violated the terms and violated its offensive program in this domain. Russia is also signator of the Chemical Weapons Convention, but "financial and other difficulties have been an impediment to the timely destruction of its chemical stockpile." ("Russia." www.nti.org May 2017)

Russian capability across the spectrum of weapons of mass destruction invoke justified concern when we observe Putin "talking casually about using nuclear weapons" ("The threat from Russia." The Economist. October 22, 2016). The international community cannot ignore belligerent talk from Russia and must also take substantive action when Russia employs its capability to violate the integrity of any nation, including Ukraine.

As a former KGB operative, Putin has a strong understanding about ties to groups with whom the Russians had common interests around the world. This understanding comes with an aggressive mindset.

In addition, for all the insults hurled at him from various corners of the globe, Vladimir Putin is perhaps one of the most secure national leaders in the world. He is as secure leading Russia as Leonid Brezhnev was leading the Soviet Union, and arguably more so. Anne Applebaum had suggested Putin would only remain in office until 2024 (Putinism: The Ideology. London School of Economics: London, 2013), but Putin's strategy of "tag-team" trading of political offices with Dmitri Medvedev, and success amending the Russian constitution suggest Putin preeminence well past 2030.

Alexei Novalny has proven an annoying opponent. In spite spending time in jail-- and a poisoning in the summer of 2020-- Novalny has inspired protests in over a hundred cities along with international condemnation. These efforts have eroded the popularity of Putin's "United Russia" party, but Putin has successfully emerged from opposition in the past with forceful arrests and patience.

Thus, we might postulate changes in policy should leadership change in Russia, due to his durability (including the amendments to the Russian constitution adopted via referendum in 2020, allowing Putin to run for two more 6-year presidential terms) we will instead focus on understanding Vladimir Putin instead. Putin's security in his role, his age and health, and his freedom of action in leadership, imply that Vladimir Putin will sit at the helm in Russia for decades. We suggest understanding Putin is more important than addressing various other factors within Russia.

© Saul Loeb/AFP/Getty Images

How does Vladimir Putin think about policy and what are his objectives? Presumably Putin's objectives are aligned with what is best for Russia, or at least what he thinks is best for Russia, within the context of his world view.

Vladimir Putin observations during the final years of the Soviet Union have resulted in specific activities. Putin has reformed the Russian Army and the Air Force (as well as the Navy), not from a theoretical perspective, but specifically due to Russian military activity in Chechnya and Georgia, Poland and the Czech Republic, as well as, more recently, Syria and Ukraine.

Soviet aid to Afghanistan began in 1979 after a pro-Soviet government took power in 1978, attempting radical reforms and alienating, then arresting many traditional Muslim Afghans across the country. After an appeal to Brezhnev, the 40th Guard Army deployed to the country and installed socialist Babrak Karmal in a coup. (Wikipedia) The Islamic Council called for immediate withdrawal of troops, while the United Nations also condemned the attack. Aid poured into the country from all corners of the globe, including from the United States CIA and a wealthy young Saudi expat with Yemeni roots named Osama bin Laden.

Vladimir Putin evidently supported Gorbachev's decision to withdraw the Soviet military presence from Afghanistan in 1991. He spoke in favor of United States action there after the 9/11 attacks in New York City, and even went on record supporting Hamid Karzai interest in increasing United States military presence in the country as recently as 2014, calling for the U.S to take responsibility for defeating the Taliban, which he felt was in Russia's best interest.

Clashes in Chechnya began well before the Communists seized control, with Stalin forcibly deporting many in the country (reportedly resulting in 25% fatalities), but Kruschev allowing resettlement. Chechnya declared independence upon the dissolution of the Soviet Union in 1991, resulting in Russian troops "restoring order" in the first Chechen war, which ended in a 1996 Khasavyurt ceasefire agreement.

Tension between Chechnya and Russia continued, both due to actions (kidnappings and other armed Dagestan activities) inside Chechnya but also because of Chechen bombings in Russia. Putin's decisive action against Chechen terrorists including both air and land wars against Chechnya were popular in Russia and contributed substantially to Putin's initial electoral success after Yeltsin stepped down from the Presidency. Russia maintains security forces in the region at this writing.

The style of Russian occupation of Ukraine in 2014 is not new. Just as Russia declared Crimea and Donbass regions of Russian nationality and interest, occupying them in 2014, Russia occupied South Ossetia and Abkhazia in the 2008 war with Georgia. In his book, A Little War that Shook the World, Ronald Asmus sketched parallels between Ukraine and Georgian passion to join NATO (and the European Union) as well as NATO/European Union reluctance to allow such expansion.

Although France's Sarkozy stepped in to mediate for Georgia (perhaps preventing Russian subjugation of Tbilisi and the government of Georgia itself), diplomacy was unable to push Russian troops back out of those regions that had been a part of Georgia. Russia retains control of the two "autonomous" regions today.

In 2014, Russia made several incursions into Ukrainian territory. Beginning with Crimea, Russian soldiers with unmarked uniforms took control of strategic positions and infrastructure within the Ukrainian territory of Crimea, which Russia annexed after a disputed referendum. Subsequently, demonstrations by pro-Russian groups in the Donbass area of Ukraine escalated into an armed conflict between the Ukrainian government and separatist forces of the self-declared Donetsk and Lugansk People's Republics. In August, Russian military vehicles crossed the border in several locations of Donetsk Oblast. The incursion by the Russian military was seen as responsible for the defeat of Ukrainian forces in early September.

When asked whether there are circumstances under which Russia will relinquish Crimea and <the naval port> Sevastopol in a 2018

interview, Putin answered, "You must be joking…." ("Putin - The Documentary…," March 24, 2018).

##

According to a former Pentagon strategy adviser there were as many as 7,000 Russian troops inside Ukraine in early November 2014, and (as mentioned earlier) OSCE monitors stated they observed vehicles transporting ammunition and soldiers' dead bodies crossing the Russian-Ukrainian border under the guise of humanitarian aid convoys. As of early August 2015, OSCE observed over 21 such vehicles marked with the Russian military code for soldiers killed in action. According to *The Moscow Times* Russia has tried to intimidate and silence human rights workers discussing Russian soldiers' deaths in the conflict. OSCE repeatedly reported that its observers were denied access to the areas controlled by "combined Russian-separatist forces".

The majority of members of the international community and organizations such as Amnesty International have condemned Russia for its actions in post-revolutionary Ukraine, accusing it of breaking international law and violating Ukrainian sovereignty. Many countries implemented economic sanctions against Russia, Russian individuals or companies – to which Russia responded in kind. (all above from Wikipedia)

■ Russian military bases
Determined by Washington Post analysis*

● NATO released satellite imagery
Released April 10 and 11

BELARUS

Western Military District

Central Military District

Base near Belgorod
1 • Belgorod

2 Buturlinovka Air Base

★ Kiev

Kharkiv •

UKRAINE

RUSSIA

Note: Bases verified through satellite image analysis and can include abandoned airfields, storage facilities and restricted areas.

Dnieper

Dnipropetrovsk •

Luhansk •

Donetsk •

Volgodonsk ■

Kuzminka 4   3 Novocherkassk
• Rostov

Melitopol •

Southern Military District

Odessa   • Kherson

5 Yeysk

Sea of Azov

0   100
MILES

6 Primorko-Akhtarsk Air Base

CRIMEA

Kerch

Simferopol

Sevastopol •

Novorossiysk •

Black Sea

If Russia has yet to occupy the remainder of Georgia (over ten years after seizing control of some parts of the territory), why are Polish, Lithuanian, Latvian and Estonians concerned that Russian forces may rework international borders again at some time in the future? Why argue here that Russia will occupy the rest of Ukraine?

128

Several reasons present themselves. First: the Communist Belorussian country immediately to Ukraine's north maintains strong ties to Russia; including a southern half of the Belorussian buffer appeals to Putin. Military experts suggest there are two "avenues of approach" from Russia to Europe… the northern "Suwalki" avenue, and the southern "Ukraine" avenue.

Suwalki and Ukraine Avenues of Approach

While the United States has provided anti-tank missiles to Ukraine to protect against a Russian armored attack, the newest Russian tank (the T14 Armata) has countermeasures that appear to make the weapon quite impervious to most anti-tank missiles. Many military experts will suggest that the best countermeasure for a tank is another tank (or perhaps the American A10 "Warthog" close air support aircraft).

A second reason for Putin's interest in controlling more of Ukraine: mineral deposits in Donbass and oil reserves immediately off the coast of Crimea may appeal to Putin the most, manufacturing capabilities remain superior in Dnipropetrovsk and Kharkiv for certain products, while oil/gas reserves in the Black Sea will belong to Ukraine, not Russia, if Putin doesn't seize the rest of the country.

The third reason for Russian interest in tighter control: Ukraine reluctance to follow the Russian lead regarding trade priorities in a European context will prove unacceptable to Putin over time.

Cursory review of Russian forces suggests that the 58th Guards Army have the resources to seize Kiev, while the 20th Guards Army (including its 3rd Motorized Rifle Division, 136th Motorized Rifle Brigade and perhaps help from the 90th Guards Tank Division) would seize eastern Ukraine through Karkhiv, Dnipropetrovsk and Zaporizhya.

We can anticipate assets from the 49th Guards Army, such as the 61st Marine Brigade and 200th Motorized Rifle Brigade, would have assistance from various Spetsnaz units, to seize the western regions north of Odessa to Kiev and Lviv.

Ukraine resources resisting aggression from Russia would be overwhelmed with such a concentration.

To date, the United States has refused to establish any stronger policy than economic sanctions against Russia for its adventurism in Ukraine. Given that those policies have not resulted in restoration of Crimea and the Donbass to Ukraine, they are unlikely to stop Russia from additional military expansion into Ukraine when the time is ripe. Can the USA do more for Ukraine?

United States Policy

This chapter will review United States policy regarding Ukraine under a lens of germs, religion, economics and ethics. We will examine the foundations of the democracy in the United States of America and (finally) propose substantive assistance to the Ukraine democracy. While this author won't suggest that Russia and surrogates be forced to vacate Ukrainian Donbass and Crimean regions (or lose military personnel and equipment in those areas under hostile fire), we suggest U. S. policing forces similar to those that have kept Communist China and North Korea from occupying the South Korean democracy since the end of hostilities in 1955.

Specifically, we suggest two United States Army Brigade Combat Teams, three Air Force squadrons and (to administer the presence) a division headquarters.

##

At this writing, we have passed the one year anniversary of an outbreak of a global pandemic. Certainly, an appropriate time to once again quote Diamond's Guns, Germs, and Steel, this time with some focus on germs. "The major killers of humanity throughout our recent history – smallpox, flu, tuberculosis, malaria, plague, measles, and cholera—are infectious diseases that evolved from diseases of animals…" (p. 197). Today's COVID illness has derived from wet markets… a third world phenomenon where slaughtered animals (in this case bats) are presented in unrefrigerated and unprocessed form, for customers to purchase, and even consume.

Diamond's book observes how these decimating diseases made the leap from animals to humans, then became "almost confined to humans." (p. 197) Diamond further observes that "over the course of history, human populations repeatedly exposed to a particular pathogen have come to consist of a higher proportion of individuals with those genes for resistance…." (201) Ultimately, the book concludes that animal domestication in Europe exposed populations there to diseases, enabling predominant survival of those with resistant genes. Without similar resistance, populations on continents without such resistance were wiped out.

Of course, the indigenous populations that European diseases destroyed did not have the advantages of modern medicine, any ability to isolate carriers of the disease, or to develop a vaccine. We hope Western Europe and North America are able to respond with science, while African, South American and Asian populations may enjoy better natural immunity to COVID due to "wet markets" in those regions.

Dr. Anthony Fauci, the public health official who survived a transition from the Trump to the Biden administrations, calls for the population to insure we receive vaccines, not only to fight the vulnerability to COVID on an individual level, but also to avoid being a host for a mutating virus. He argues that widespread vaccination will dramatically reduce the ability for the virus to survive and persist via mutation for this reason.

But what does this have to do with Ukraine? One word: priorities. Just as a conversation about Hunter Biden's involvement with Ukrainian natural gas firm Burisma were reaching a fever pitch and the impeachment of Donald Trump had stalled, the pandemic emerged to capture headlines and dominate both policy and media programming in the United States.

##

In a nation where we claim to separate church and state, and the party that has come to dominate legislative and executive branches of government takes a decidedly anti-religious perspective, Judeo-Christian perspectives seem to dominate the focus of our Defense Department.

Muslims are obliged to obey only God's command in the holy Koran to wage jihad against the occupiers of Muslim lands until final victory and liberation. (Foreign Broadcast Information Service— Near East and South Asia, March 5, 1996, p. 87)

Best not to fulfill the prophesies of a holy text, if possible. Yet this is what United States policy has achieved in our attacks on Al Qaida and, subsequently, ISIS. Between the year 2000 and the first publication of this book, the United States spent over $1.5 trillion for actions in Afghanistan and Iraq. The United States had already spent over $8 billion fighting ISIS and was spending over $600,000 AN HOUR against ISIS at that time (www.nationalpriorities.org).

There were about 20,000 vehicles in Afghanistan when the Obama administration drawdown began. Roughly half were still there in 2015 with plans for disposal for another 5,000 happening that year (US World Report). 2.4 million pieces of equipment worth a total of at least $250 million -- everything from tanks <including the entire 2d Armored Cavalry Regiment, at the time, 2/3 of a Heavy Division> and trucks to office furniture and latrines -- were left with the Iraqi government in 2011.

Policy makers have NOT been arguing for a forward presence of American equipment or Soldiers in Ukraine.

…the U.S. Armed Forces will … <defend> the homeland; <conduct> sustained, distributed counterterrorist operations; and … <deter> aggression … through forward

presence and engagement.
United States 2014 <u>Quadrennial</u> <u>Defense</u> <u>Review</u>, p. 12.

Focus on counterterrorist operations has had a number of first, second and third order effects on United States military operations, and of course, on military capability. Our forces are agile, able to strike precision targets in forbidding international locations, and responsive to collection of individual "criminal type" activities on a global scale. Unfortunately, these capabilities and focus are not conducive to countering a large national force, from nations such as China or Russia.

While the most likely Chinese adventurism involves naval operations across the South China Sea and Taiwan Strait, Russian adventurism has already begun in Ukraine.

Timing of Russia's intervention in Ukraine was driven by events there, and not to take advantage of the US Quadrennial Defense strategy cycle, but the investment that the Defense Department makes in the Quadrennial Review and the momentum that the document requires as a result, are not insignificant. Timing for Putin's Russia was fortuitous.

In June 2014, a few months after the publication of the United States Quadrennial Review, and in response to Putin's Ukraine adventurism, President Obama proposed a European Reassurance Initiative in Warsaw. This initiative shifted resources to Europe, including Army and Air Force support to NATO and Navy presence in Black and Baltic Seas, as well as Marine activity in Romania and Bulgaria and "prepositioning additional stocks of equipment in Europe." (European Reassurance Initiative (DOD Budget FY2017, dated February 2016, p.6).

Much to Russia's chagrin, destroyer USS Porter arrived in Varna, Bulgaria, via the Black Sea, on June 9, 2016. ("Russia vows response," Navy Times: June 10, 2016)

President Recep Tayyip Erdogan of Turkey, a NATO ally, said he complaiined to NATO Secretary General Jens Stoltenberg that the alliance needed to do more in the Black Sea to prevent Russian dominance in the area, the U.S. Naval Institute reported. (Ibid)

"I told him 'You are absent from the Black Sea,' " Erdogan said in an address to Balkan military leaders. "The Black Sea has almost become a Russian lake. If we don't act now, history will not forgive us." (Ibid) Under the terms of the 1936 Montreux Convention, non-Black Sea countries can have no more than 9 warships in the Black Sea at one time and each ship must leave after 21 days. (Ibid)

On May 2014, in response to a referendum within Crimea which resulted in Russian annexation of the territory, President Obama announced sanctions on individuals in Putin's staff and others supporting the Russian government. The President called the referendum and annexation a clear violation of the Ukraine constitution and international law.

Thus, President Obama imposed sanctions on a handful of officials of the Russian government, as well as on the Russian arms industry, and on individuals or entities that acts on behalf of the subjects of the boycott.

##

The world was a very different geopolitical puzzle in 1990. The Soviet Union was a year from crumbling, but very much perceived to have a relevant political philosophy that still resonated with the repressed, downtrodden and idealistic. Mikhail Gorbachev was popular around the world and his ideas for perestroika were compelling for many. The lesson of Nicholas II navy had caught hold: if you tighten decisions to the very top, at best good decisions will be slow in coming... at worst, resources will be wasted while vast and exciting new opportunities will go unattended.

For the thirty years leading to 1990, the United States had come from the robust Gross National Product and foreign exchange of trade with 7% growth in oil consumption and a 5% economic growth rate, to the phase from 1973 to 1975, when the US consumed 6% less oil and suffered a 6% economic decline.

From 1975 to 1979 US oil consumption rate resumed a growth
rate at about 6% per year while the economy grew at 5.5% per
year. In 1979 another set of oil price shocks set in, inspiring
significant oil conservation policies. Thus:

> From 1979 to 1982, US oil consumption declined at an in-
> credible 5% per year, with no growth in the economy during
> that period, and a major recession set in.(http://www.hub-
> bertpeak.com/reynolds/sovietdecline.htm)

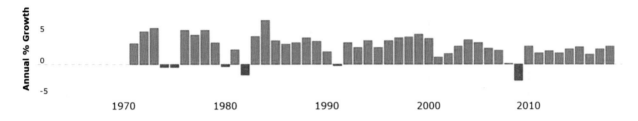

https://www.macrotrends.net/countries/USA/united-states/gnp-gross-national-product

The long gas lines of the Carter administration had a dramatic impact on the US economy, and were a fresh memory several
years later, when George Bush was elected President. Bush had
run for various offices in Texas, but lost in each bid, while
his involvement at senior levels of the US government (including
responsibility for the CIA during the Nixon administration) had
refined the President's global view and understanding of United
States options.

The recently concluded war with Iran had left Iraq's Sunni
Ba'athist dictator, Saddam Hussein, with substantial financial

obligations coming due, while Kuwait and the UAE were overpro-
ducing oil, driving down prices across the Middle East. Unfortunately (for Saddam Hussein), Jordan and Egypt were unsympa-
thetic to Iraq's financial challenges.

The Iraqi Army — then the 4th largest in the world -- had
some of the Soviet Union's best ground weapon systems while
world leadership and United States intelligence community agreed
Saddam Hussein's Iraq also possessed nuclear and chemical weapons. It was this Iraqi force that, on August 2, 1990, invaded
Kuwait.

George Bush rapidly built consensus among US allies around
the world for a full-scale intervention and placed a massive
force that easily rolled over Saddam's paper tiger. Since US
analysts projected this stunning defeat would result in Saddam's
overthrow in due course, the President opted to withdraw US
Forces after declaring victory but without destroying some of
Saddam's most elite forces.

Shortly after US forces withdrew from Iraq, the Soviet Union collapsed. A widely heralded "peace dividend" drove dramatic reductions in United States force structure. At the same
time, Ukraine and the rest of Eastern Europe transferred nuclear
weapons to Russia, at a time that non-proliferation experts felt
such consolidation would provide better control of those weapons.

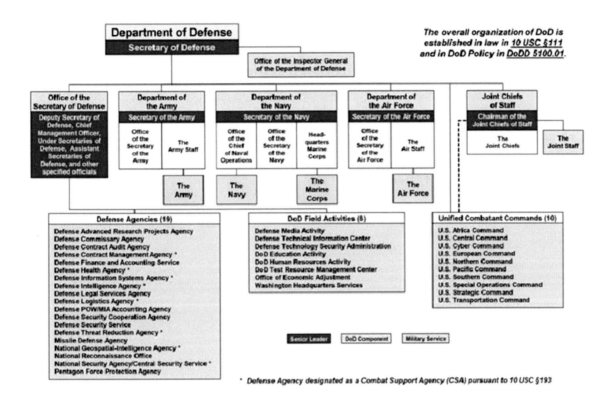

The United States Department of Defense

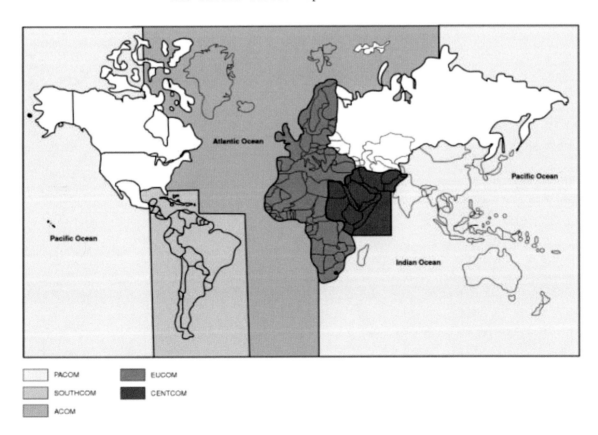

Due to the passing of its long-time, charismatic leader Josip Broz Tito, in 1980, Yugoslavia had begun to fracture, but the collapse of the Soviet Union in 1991 enabled a complete power vacuum. (Alan Axelrod, America's Wars. Wiley & Sons: New York, 2002, p. 509). Serbian president Slobodan Milosevic vowed to protect the Serbian minority in Bosnia. Global sanctions against the Milosevic government didn't stop ethnic cleansing of Muslims and Croats, although NATO involvement (led by the United States) did.

Then in late 2001, a coordinated team of Islamic terrorists hijacked four jetliners, successfully flying two of them into the World Trade Center towers in New York City and a third into the Pentagon, while a fourth airliner went down in a field in Pennsylvania after passengers stormed the terrorists on the plane.

As outlined earlier, George W. Bush's father (and advisors) were convinced Saddam Hussein's humiliating defeat would inspire the collapse of his regime. This was not what transpired, and after the 9/11 terrorist attack, US senior leadership argued that Saddam's residual (and growing) nuclear capability made it the most threatening of the Mideast nation states.

George W. Bush's team (including former Joint Chief of Staff GEN Colin Powell) launched another attack on Iraq, resulting in the decisive defeat of Saddam Hussein and, ultimately, Saddam's capture and execution. Unexpectedly, Saddam's forces melted into Iraqi cities and towns, in a resistance inspired by Muhammed's warning about foreign occupiers.

The Iraq Study Group Report (Baker and Hamilton) provided 79 recommendations for addressing the challenge there, including a resolution that the US does not want permanent bases in Iraq (#22) and that the US does not want to control Iraq's oil (#23).

In the vacuum left when Saddam's vicious and controlling apparatus collapsed, various Muslim groups and militias formed. In the months after the United States occupation, these groups became increasingly well organized and increasingly radicalized. US DOD leadership realized, from company grade to flag level, that the environment they were attempting to control, was as complex and challenging as any a younger Army, and earlier Department of Defense, had faced in Vietnam.

Although Muhammed managed to formulate the new Muslim faith, establish a set of laws governing most aspects of life and dominate Arabia politically, after his death in 632AD, his followers quickly divided into two camps: 1) those who felt the theocracy should be governed by those with appropriate religious credentials (Shia); and 2) those who felt leadership must be de-scended from Muhammed (Sunni).

In the socialist and communist movements that swept the world in the 1920's and 1930's, the Ba'ath Party emerged with its distinctive Arab flavor in the Mideast. Sunni leaders such as Saddam Hussein in Iraq tapped Ba'ath ideology to court other Socialist support (especially the Soviet Union) and to subsume the sectarian flavor in his ruthless activities to maintain control of his country. Shia leaders such as al-Assad in Syria claimed allegiance to Ba'ath principles for the same reason.

Although Ba'ath party members continue to survive and, indeed, lead governments or paramilitary organizations in Syria and Iraq today, purely sectarian disputes motivate the internal conflict in those countries, while fueling the bloodiest anti-American fervor as well.

David Petraeus was able to clarify US forces mission in 2007 and, through a surge of forces, bring order for a time (Thomas E. Ricks, The Gamble. Penguin Press: New York, 2009). Unfortunately, some years later, "… a stable Iraq that is uni-fied, at peace with its neighbors, and is able to police its internal affairs, so it isn't a sanctuary for al Qaeda," (IBID p. 316) has yet to arrive.

Although US forces tended to generalize about the sectarian conflict (attributing much activity to al Qaida before finding

144

and killing Osama bin Laden; and much activity to ISIS afterward), the violence from the radical Muslim community has been at best a multi-headed snake; at worst, a constantly ebbing and flowing pit of vipers that spread through Iraq, Syria, Afghanistan, the Federally Administered Tribal Areas (FATA) of Pakistan, and beyond.

##

Special Operations are not new to the United States military. Roger's Rangers were operating in New England before the US Revolutionary War, and every conflict from then until the present day had Soldiers who fit the description. That said, the scope of the failure (and the systemic nature of the problems) of the team Jimmy Carter asked to rescue Americans captured in Tehran inspired Ronald Reagan to create a unified Special Operations Command before the end of his term of office.

> Born of a failed 1980 raid to rescue American hostages in Iran (in which eight US service members died), US Special Operations Command was established in 1987. Made up of units from all the service branches, SOCOM is tasked with carrying out Washington's most specialized and secret missions, including assassinations, counterterrorist raids, special reconnaissance, unconventional warfare, psychological operations, foreign troop training, and weapons of mass destruction counter-proliferation operations. Nick Turse. "The Startling Size of US Special Operations," Mother Jones. September/October 2016.

Reagan had created the command to improve coordination and ensure appropriate assets were designed and acquired to support unique requirements that might arise. Today's Special Forces

145

are not only tightly integrated across the service arms (Navy, Air Force, Army) but also coordinate closely with more departments and bureaus of the United States government than the average reader is aware even exist.

Special Operations missions range from training foreign fighters or police to precision rescues and attacks like the one that buried Osama bin Laden at sea. Staffing grew from 33,000 in 2001 to 72,000 in 2014, while funding went from $2.3B to over $7B. (Ibid.) To put this growth in perspective, during this period, overall DOD funding grew from $380B to over $500B, although DOD headcount dropped somewhat overall.

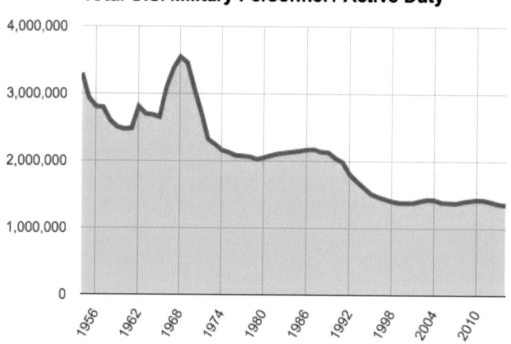

David Coleman, US Military Personnel 1954-2014,
www.historyinpeices.com

In addition to the unified nature of SOCOM planning, efforts leverage a dramatic new player in modern war: the Unmanned Air Vehicle, or UAV. Although these vehicles began as intelligence devices, soon after the start of the Iraq war, the Pentagon modified UAV's to be able to carry precision guided munitions, which could be dispatched when cameras suggested/confirmed a high value target was in range.

> An August 2013, Brookings Institution study reported that in the U.S. Air Force there were approximately 1,300 remotely piloted aircraft (RPA) pilots, 8.5 percent of total Air Force pilots, up from 3.3 percent in 2008… <but> that the U.S. military's … missions requirement is growing at a faster pace than RPA pilots can be trained…
> (Wikipedia)

Although UAV strike capability may have been instrumental in the decline of al Qaida, these vehicles and the "kill capability" they represent are fraught with policy challenges. Detailed coordination to reach into a foreign county isn't as necessary as larger airspace incursions or "boots on the ground" insertions. Attacks seem also more prone to erroneous targeting or civilian casualties.

The trends, however, are unmistakable. Even as early as mid-2014, the US Air Force was training more UAV pilots than fighter and bomber pilots combined.

##

The UAV is not the only new development in the conduct of war. Just as information technology and the internet have dramatically transformed private commerce and the way governments provide services, some of the most highly publicized incidents associated with modern American war have involved information technology, the methods that modern data is stored, and the vulnerabilities that an increasingly electronic world presents to would be attackers, whether those attackers represent nation states or non-state organizations.

A low level IT administrator, working with Wikileaks infrastructure and it's mastermind, Julian Assange, exposes classified data to audiences much larger than ever before possible with Bradley/Chelsea Manning following suit. Of course, spies have been a component of wars from the beginning, but IT and the internet magnify the damage (or at least embarrassment) a single actor can cause.

In the words of Shane Harris, author of @War: the Rise of the Military Internet Complex:

> …references to Snowden, seeing him as neither whistle-blowing hero nor treasonous narcissist: *It turned out that the NSA, which wanted to protect computers from Wall Street to the water company, couldn't keep a twenty-nine year-old contractor from making off with the blueprints to its global surveillance system.*

Although illegal and subject to international and very vocal complaints (recall reaction to Russian hacking of Democratic convention messaging), hacking has become a part of government, business and even personal life. Shane emphasizes, "nearly everybody is spying on and hacking everybody else." (Ibid)

##

Combat has changed, and Russia is no longer a backwater power in any respect. Although the Russian economy may not rival United States or Chinese volumes, Putin plans to drive an agenda, and he doesn't hesitate to use force, oil/gas shipments or other mechanism for driving Russian interests forward. How should the United States respond?

In his book, A Little War that Shook the World, Ron Asmus does an excellent job outlining NATO and European Union reluctance to welcome Ukraine, although his focus is on the nation of Georgia. His description of French involvement in the ceasefire contradicts Marin Katusa's assessment in his book, The Colder War, (Wiley & Sons: New York, 2015) which suggests the Swiss brokered the cease fire in the Georgian conflict with Russia. In any event, both accounts acknowledge that a cease fire has left Russia occupying parts of what had been Georgia, and that Vladimir Putin will strongly oppose further expansion of NATO and the European Union to welcome Ukraine, even if those two organizations were willing to accept the Nation's western aspirations, which they do not.

The United States is not politically positioned to "steam-roll" Ukraine membership of NATO, or its membership of the European Union. Russia will tolerate a strong, independent nation at its border. The consensus view is: Russia's historic inferiority complex prevents allowing Ukraine (or other nations like Georgia or Belarus) attain true independence.

Marin Katusa attributes the success of Ukraine's Maidan revolution (and the successful election of Petro Poroshenko to Ukraine's presidency) to United States involvement (Ibid., pp. 76-77). While Europe has been heavily involved insuring Ukraine elections are not rigged, Ukraine voter cynicism about Ukraine oligarch behavior was only suspended temporarily to elect Petro Poroshenko after Maiden. His supporters are still watching Volodimyr Zelenskiy to conclude whether his "Servant of the People" party and new Ukraine government will effectively address corruption and reinvigorate the Ukraine economy.

Given Angela Merkel's East German past, deferring to her judgement regarding the Ukraine might seem judicious. However, just as the United States learned during the Georgian crisis, a European mediator may not choose to stand toe to toe with Russia.

The content of this book must reflect the shifting winds of United States national politics. At the original writing, the 2016 presidential election was raging. Would the next president be Hillary or The Donald? Although Hillary Clinton emerged from the convention period with a strong lead, momentum shifted to Republican nominee Donald Trump, after allegations regarding an unsecure email server Clinton leveraged when Secretary of State.

Hillary Clinton was integrally involved in fashioning Barack Obama's foreign policy as Secretary of State. Perhaps she would have avoided changing Obama's policies substantively: standing up to Putin in Ukraine was not on her agenda at any time during the campaign. Would President Biden bring the United States back to the policy baseline we can examine under President Obama?

Although Donald Trump hired a top campaign aid with heavy Ukraine involvement, Trump's announced policies never suggested he would stand up to Putin over Ukraine (and his aid with Ukraine experience was fired/stepped down due to allegations of corruption during his tenure in Ukraine). During the campaign, Donald Trump argued for a purer "anti-terror" policy than did Hillary Clinton and explored dropping sanctions imposed upon Russia regarding Ukraine.

Focus of United States efforts regarding weapons of mass destruction ("WMD") were consistent with Donald Trump's long-standing anti-terror approach. The Department of Homeland Defense has rapidly built systems for identifying and addressing methods a terrorist organization or single actor might take to deploy WMD against the United States.

Perhaps the most concerning rebuttal to a "boots on the ground" peace keeping response to Russia's Ukrainian aspirations is threat of WMD attack from Russia. Weapons of mass destruction are a new phenomena… certainly not envisioned when the founding fathers framed the United States Constitution.

##

While the credibility of the United States Constitution certainly resonates with large swathes of the American public, without an understanding of its history and the background its framers brought to its composition, we might simply call the document a glorious accident. Of course, almost any occurrence might be called a glorious accident (or act of God, from another perspective), given origins of factors leading to the result, but the factors are interesting here.

Founders of the United States Constitution were very well educated for that time, and indeed, in the context of almost any group we might examine in history. Thought leaders at the Constitutional Conventions were steeped in the science of the day, and also aware of the latest political thought: Voltaire ("Discourse on Inequality," "The Social Contract," and other works), Rousseau, Locke, Descarte were all familiar and influential.

George Washington, the hero and military leader of the Revolution, chaired the convention, while Benjamin Franklin (at 81 years) was the sage in the group. James Madison took copious notes and later introduced 19 amendments in Congress, 12 of which were sent to the original states for ratification,

10 of which were ratified to become the United States Bill of Rights.

Debate regarding the adoption of the Constitution and subsequent Bill of Rights raged between Federalists and anti-Federalists, with compromise driving the ultimate shape of the document and resulting government. A balance of powers between the executive branch, the legislative branch and the judiciary were intended to keep the Federal government from overstepping its bounds.

The framers were representatives from all walks of life: merchants, farmers, bankers and lawyers. Many had served in the Continental Army, colonial legislatures or in the Continental

Congress. 8 were signers of the Declaration of Independence, while 6 had signed the Articles of Confederation, which were deemed too weak to hold the new nation together.

The Constitution has mechanisms for censuring bad or corrupt behavior of elected officials, largely through impeachment. The framers maintained a certain collegiality towards one another, even as they disagreed (in some cases dramatically so) about fundamentals regarding how the government ought to be shaped.

##

Donald Trump was elected on a platform that included "draining the swamp" in Washington. We can probably all agree he was not successful in doing so. Democrats and "Never-Trumper" Republicans may have been concerned a Trump agenda wouldn't drain any swamp, but simply replace theirs with his.

Certainly, any reader who tuned in for the first impeachment hearings of Donald Trump, or who reads books such as COMPROMISED: Counterintelligence and the Threat of Donald Trump by Peter Strzok (Houghton Mifflin Harcourt: New York, 2020) or The Impeachment Report: the House Intelligence Committee's Report on its Investigation into Donald Trump and Ukraine by Jon Meacham (Random House Books: New York, 2019) can hardly avoid strong discomfort with claims of witnesses, and in some cases, with the conduct of supposedly loyal public servants. Yet

taking into consideration that Hunter Biden and business

associates (even relatives) of Mitt Romney (to name only two)

were involved in Ukraine business dealings (presumably highly

profitable and hinging on an impression that personal

relationships would help deliver results), we may wonder what

financial transactions may have transpired had Donald Trump not

shown a bright light on Ukraine, with his phone call to

President Zelenskiy.

The reader, and, indeed, the Ukraine electorate, want to

believe Volodymir Zelenskiy will track down corruption, not only

among Ukrainian (and other) oligarchs, but also root out

complicity across the international business community. Sadly,

there would appear to be a fine line between legal—even

acceptable-- business and relation "quid pro quo" and an

impeachable offense. The United States electorate has a right

to expect better from our leadership—and so do Ukrainians.

##

Congress has enacted many laws to block corruption in gov-

ernment, across a broad spectrum of activities including govern-

ment acquisition. These laws (and corresponding regulations)

are codified in the Federal Acquisition Regulation, including

155

notification of the government of certain legal violations, prohibitions against false claims and actions to take in the event of overpayment. Businesses seeking contracts to provide products or services to the government are required to have a Code of Business Ethics and Conduct, even covering permissible and impermissible gifts to government employees (including buying of meals and free transportation). We will not attempt to summarize the Federal Acquisition Regulation here, but merely direct the reader's attention to it.

Recent Presidents have also signed executive orders pertaining to government ethics, including both President Biden and President Trump, although Donald Trump revoked his order (EO 13770) a few days before leaving office (as did President Bill Clinton in the remaining weeks of his administration). Biden's order requires a waiver before any registered lobbyist may join his administration and prohibits "shadow lobbying," which allowed activities for some former administration officials in recent past.

Secretary Austin with National Guard troops. Seligman and O'Brien. "Austin ousts Pentagon Advisory Board Members…," Politico, February 2, 2021.

Lobbying organizations criticize such orders claiming they remove people with "real-life experience" from consideration. Apparently the new Defense Secretary decision to suspend operations of 42 advisory panels was driven more due to Trump appointee presence on those panels than any ethics considerations. President Biden's new Defense Secretary, Lloyd Austin, is the Department's first African American in that role.

##

President Biden must stand up to Vladimir Putin in Ukraine. Perhaps underscoring the renewed power of Putin's nation and the momentum of that nation under his stewardship will help. Emphasis on the peacekeeping nature of United States efforts and the conventional make-up of any Ukraine deployment must remain paramount. United States "boots on the ground" in Ukraine must stand in the way of Russian incursions in Kharkiv, Dnipropetrovsk and Odessa, Ukraine, and serve to reinforce economic and governmental improvement in that nation. Sanctions haven't worked… and, the United States will miss its opportunity to help once Putin has taken military control of the rest of the country.

Why Ukraine, why now?

So the strategic goal for people who want to see a more peaceful and democratic world is a Russia that, like Ukraine, wants to be democratic and a part of Europe. Right now such a scenario seems very unlikely. But if Ukraine succeeds, there is the possibility for a better outcome. That is why Ukraine's struggle for democracy, independence, and territorial integrity has consequences for the whole world. And it's why the US has a profound stake in its success. By standing with Ukraine, we are not merely supporting its struggle. We are also defending our own national security and advancing the values of human freedom that America, with all its troubles, continues to represent. Carl Gershman, "A Fight for Democracy: Why Ukraine Matters." World Affairs. March/April 2015.

While deploying the 1st Armored Division from Ft Hood to Ukraine (accompanying it with one squadron each of A10 aircraft

F15's and F16's) would be ideal, such a move would be tremendously expensive and take time. The 1st Armored Division would supplement Ukraine defenses of Kiev with an Armored Brigade, provide Karkhiv with an Armored Brigade and help defend east of Dnipropetrovsk with a Stryker Brigade.

A quicker implementation (and smaller footprint deployment) would include tasking the XVIII Corps (ABN) with a seven day "WARNO" to defend at Chuihuiv (at least two companies) and Stari Saltiv (at least one company) with the 2/503 Inf BN from Vicenza, and also giving the Rapid Reaction Brigade 30 days to move from Fort Bragg to Karkhiv. In this scenario, the Second Cavalry Regiment can be tasked to move from Vilseck Germany to defend east of Zaporizhya, while the squadron of A10's can be based in support, perhaps in Krivyi Rih (adjustments have been made to force allocation since this writing, but we leave the original form for practicality's sake). Two Air Force fighter squadrons can support US infrastructure with air cover and additional ground support, perhaps a squadron each in Kiev (F16's) and Lviv (F15's), just as they would in a 1st Armored Division scenario.

The XVIII Corps (ABN) can be tasked to provide a DISCOM to Ukraine (operating from Kiev) to support an American Army footprint there (and a US air force logistical "tail" for A10 and F16 units), with its Rapid Reaction Brigade and 2/503 relieved with a national guard BCT within six months. Perhaps the 2d Cavalry is replaced in Vilsec with the 3d Cavalry, projecting a rotation of units in Ukraine at one year out.

The second scenario leaves ground defense of Kiev to Ukraine forces, with support from the F16 squadrons, should Russia choose a tactical expansion into Ukraine. Ramifications for sourcing aircraft and ground vehicle parts from Ukraine promise a strong inject to the Ukraine economy, with cost savings also expected for the US defense budget, although savings might not exceed the added expense of placing this infrastructure in Ukraine.

##

Foreign governments might well criticize the United States for meddling in their affairs without getting our own in order. Indeed, the gap between its richest and poorest has continued to grow in the United States, in spite of the best efforts of the two term Democratic President before President Trump, to extend health care to all, and ensure a robust economy that can deliver a reasonable livelihood to all willing to work for it.

Some would argue that access to capital has grown more challenging in a world where social media affords the opportunity to publish for low cost and publicize for nothing. Yet the net result of these low costs is that every message fills the air waves and often our streets, where reality television dominates our programming and even drives selection of a major party presidential candidate.

Our democracy has the world's record as the longest running government so formed, but dominance of the two major parties, works in conjunction with tight "elite" control over candidate selection to frustrate many US citizens, even if "elite Republicans" weren't able to stop a Donald Trump campaign for the nomination. Party machinery dominates selection of national representatives and selection of candidates at state and local government levels, while gerrymandering insures most congressional seats are safe (for either one party or the other). Thus, although voter anger with Congress is at all-time highs, ability to defeat a Congressman or woman is not.

The United States Constitution was approved to ensure much governance occurs at the local level, but the net result are a mishmash of local counties, cities and towns whose processes are a mystery to most, even most local citizenry. Once a citizen learns the process, he or she is often confronted with entrenched interests that protect local establishments and fight both economic growth and positive change.

While voter turnout for United States mid-term elections in 2014 were lower than any election since 1942, percentage of eligible voters turning out for the 2020 presidential election was higher than any election since 1900, when 73.7% of the eligible vote cast ballots. (Schaul, Rabinowitz and Mellnick. "2020 Turnout is the Highest in over a century," Washington Post. November 5, 2020.)

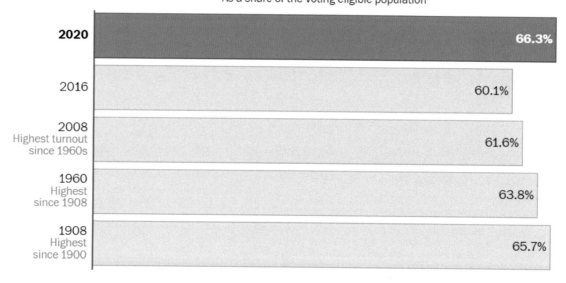

How 2020 compares to other high-turnout presidential elections
As a share of the voting-eligible population

2020	**66.3%**
2016	60.1%
2008 Highest turnout since 1960s	61.6%
1960 Highest since 1908	63.8%
1908 Highest since 1900	65.7%

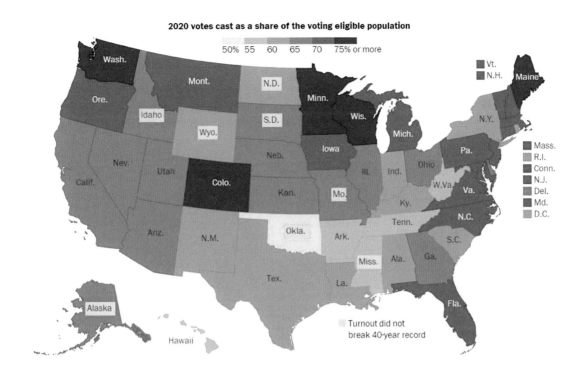

2020 votes cast as a share of the voting eligible population

50% 55   60   65   70   75% or more

Turnout did not
break 40-year record

Perhaps important to consider regarding voter turnout:
women, Asian American and many native Americans weren't permit-
ted to vote at the last turnout record, and African Americans,
although legally eligible, were in many cases prevented from
voting due to Jim Crow laws and other pressures. (Ibid.)

##

If we argue here that helping improve government and security in Ukraine is worth effort and perhaps American lives, certainly, improving government and prosperity in these United
States is similarly worthy.

We encourage you to get involved in your local government. Make things better helping those in office, or run for office yourself. "With liberty and justice for all" remains a worthy pursuit, also a challenge that one or two policy adjustments cannot deliver without consensus and ethical pursuit. This is your government, your world. Take part in it!

About the Author

P. Phillips Godston received the Julius Turner Prize for work in Political Science as an undergraduate at The Johns Hopkins University. Godston was commissioned in the U. S. Army upon graduation from Hopkins, serving as a Regular Army officer in Korea and Germany. He left active duty to attend Harvard Business School, where he received an MBA in 1989. Since then Pete has worked for numerous tech, consulting and government contracting firms, including Sun Microsystems, Software Emancipation, Spacenet, Lockheed Martin and CACI International. He continued his service through the National Guard and Reserves, including leading a battalion-sized task force in Iraq, retiring from the Army Reserves in 2011. Pete lives near his two daughters in Virginia, where he is working on a cloud solutions start-up. This is the third edition of his second book.

Made in the USA
Middletown, DE
23 April 2021